W9-CFQ-621

THE NEXT
BIG
THING

How Little Choices
Can Make a Big Impact

WHAT OTHERS ARE SAYING ABOUT THE NEXT BIG THING:

Danny has hit this one out of the park. This is his best book yet — and they are all great. He grasps and communicates the upside-down nature of the kingdom Jesus came to set up on earth. And he writes about it without a lot of religious jargon and hype, very honest, very compelling. You won't be able to put it down.

Floyd McClung, All Nations, Cape Town, South Africa

Danny's book is a positive encouragement that there is an abundant, wonderful Christian life ahead of us — one obedient step at a time. I am different for having read this book in seeing things with the eyes of God on what is truly big.

Wayne Cordeiro, Pastor, New Hope Christian Fellowship, Honolulu, Hawaii

It is my delight to wholeheartedly endorse my dear friend Danny Lehmann's compelling, fascinating book, *The Next Big Thing.* The reason is simple. It's all about being radically real as a way of life according to God's standards from His Word, the Bible; and that's what the author's life is all about. And there's nothing dull about either of these factors. So do yourself a favor: absorb the contents and live them. Someone will say the same thing about you one day!!

Joy Dawson, Author, Speaker

Sorry to say that there are many Christian books today that are just confusing people, but this is not one of them. Danny sticks to the message of God's Word. I have known him for a long time and know that He walks the talk which for me is important. You will be challenged and helped as you read this unique, cutting edge, grace awakened visionary book.

Dr. George Verwer, Founder, Operation Mobilization

It's not easy to communicate simplicity and depth at the same time, but Danny has mastered this craft in *The Next Big Thing*. Like a good scouring pad to a crusty pan, Danny uses his own flawed self to get us to look inside our own crusty lives and cry "God clean me on the inside."

Bill Stonebraker, Pastor, Calvary Chapel, Honolulu, Hawaii

This is a great read! *The Next Big Thing* will restore joy to your soul while God has you paying attention to those small things comprising most of your life. This is a book about living a happy, carefree, and contagious life; one that can be your own!

Ralph Moore, Pastor, Hope Chapel Kaneohe Bay, Hawaii

Danny Lehmann has been a mentor to many and has lived a life of authentic pursuit of God. He is a legend when it comes to encouraging others to live by faith. *The Next Big Thing* defines godly success, sheds light on the struggle with pride, and gives instruction on how to live life with humble obedience for maximum kingdom impact. *The Next Big Thing* should be the next thing you read.

Mike Kai, Pastor, Hope Chapel West O'ahu, Hawaii

One of the key components to being used by God is to simply pay attention. In a world where so many people are consumed by making big plans in the distant future, we miss out the huge opportunities that God brings to us in our immediate present. For all practical purposes, we are living distracted lives focusing on accomplishing our BIG thing rather than doing the GOD thing that's right in front of you. It's a trap that we need to break free from! That is why, *The Next Big Thing* is a must read for anybody that wants to be used by God. It is a practical book that will help you understand that the Next Big Thing is to be faithful with WHATEVER thing God has put in your hand!

Pedro Garcia, Pastor, Calvary Chapel of Kendall, Florida

THE NEXT
BIG
THING

How Little Choices
Can Make a Big Impact

Danny Lehmann
With Scott Tompkins

Foreword by Loren Cunningham

Stoker Stuff
Honolulu, Hawaii

The Next Big Thing:
How Little Choices Can Make a Big Impact

Copyright © 2012 by Danny Lehmann

Published by Stoker Stuff
Box 61700
Honolulu, Hawaii 96839
www.stokerstuff.com

All rights reserved. No part of this publication may be reproduced, stored in a retrieval system, or transmitted in any form or by any means—electronic, mechanical, photocopy, recording, or any other—except for brief quotations in printed reviews, without the prior permission of the publisher.

Unless noted, all Scripture taken from the Holy Bible, New International Version®. Copyright © 1973, 1978, 1984, 2011 by Biblica, Inc. Used by permission of Zondervan. All rights reserved.

Scripture marked KJV taken from the Holy Bible, King James Version.

Scripture marked GNT taken from the Good News Translation® (Today's English Version, Second Edition) Copyright © 1992 American Bible Society. All rights reserved.

Scripture marked NASB taken from the New American Standard Bible®, Copyright 1960, 1962, 1963, 1968, 1971, 1972,1973,1975,1977,1995 by The Lockman Foundation. Used by permission.

Scripture marked Phillips taken from The New Testament in Modern English, Copyright © 1958, 1959, 1960 J.B. Phillips and 1947, 1952, 1955, 1957 by The Macmillian Company, New York. Used by permission. All rights reserved.

Cover Design by Michael B. Hardie, www.michaelbhardie.com
Edited by Scott Tompkins
Text Design and Print Production by
Penmar Hawaii Corporation

ISBN: 978-0-9838786-0-5

Printed in China

Dedication

In loving memory to Kevin Darrough and Kit Lauer, dear friends who went to be with the Lord during the writing of this book. They were brilliant examples of the Next-Big-Thing lifestyle.

Kevin Darrough was a convert from the Moon (Rev. Sun Myung Moon's Unification Church) to the Son (Jesus Christ). He was always doing the Next Big Thing. Kevin had a heart to reach the lost: he organized citywide "March For Jesus" outreaches in California; trained others to use performing arts for cross-cultural evangelism; his Schools for Evangelism sent many workers into the harvest. He pioneered churches and training centers in the Philippines and India. Kevin courageously battled cancer for eight years, however, whenever he had the physical energy he was on a plane to Asia and hiked Nepal's mountains to reach Tibetans for Christ. Despite his health challenges, Kevin kept us laughing with his unique sense of humor. Up until the end, he loved God and people well. Kevin left behind a legacy of changed lives. Mahalo nui loa my friend.

Dr. Kit Lauer was an associate/teaching pastor at Hope Chapel, Kihei, Maui. Truly a "ten talent" guy, Kit used his natural abilities and spiritual gifts for God's glory. Kit's keen intellect and passion for apologetics was used to equip others to offer reasonable answers to skeptics and lead them to Christ. He is also remembered for possessing a contagious, childlike love for Jesus. You are greatly missed, my brother – in Maui and beyond.

"Who can comprehend how those whom God takes so early are chosen?

Does not the early death of young Christians always appear to us as if God were plundering his own best instruments in a time in which they are most needed? Yet the Lord makes no mistakes. Might God need our brothers for some hidden service on our behalf in the heavenly world?

We should put an end to our human thoughts, which always wish to know more than they can, and cling to that which is certain. Whomever God calls home is someone God has loved.

'For their souls were pleasing to the Lord, therefore he took them quickly from the midst of a world of wickedness' (Wisdom of Solomon 4)."

Dietrich Bonhoeffer

TABLE OF CONTENTS

Acknowledgements xi

Foreword xiii

Introduction.. 1

1   Why "Little" is the Next Big Thing 5

2   Big Things and Butterfly Wings 21

3   Little Words and Big Things 41

4   Learning to Love Well 57

5   It's a Wonderful Life 71

6   Role Praying 89

7   Making History 103

8   Sweat the Small Stuff 121

9   No Little People, No Little Places 145

10   The Big Picture: What on Earth is
     The Kingdom of Heaven? 159

Acknowledgements

Special Thanks to:

My wife Linda
For helping me get this project started and living
the Next-Big-Thing lifestyle.

My faithful assistants
Meaghan Koski, Erin Burr, and Katherine Kim for typing
(and retyping!) the manuscript.

Scott Tompkins
For wielding his editing scissors with compassion.

My mentors
Loren Cunningham, Chuck Smith, Floyd McClung, Winkie
Pratney, Greg Laurie, George Verwer and Don Richardson.

My pastors
Bill Stonebraker, Mark Buckley, Garry Ansdell, and Mike Kiley.

My fellow YWAMMERS
Most of whom labor in obscurity, doing The Next Big Thing
that God puts in front of them.

The Lehmanns
Daniel and Esther (Malachi, Zane, Reiya, and Evangeline),
David and Kim (Elijah).

FOREWORD

The year was 1907, and in Pyongyang, Korea a group of missionaries were meeting together for prayer. One man felt tremendous conviction over the sin of racial pride. He stood weeping and began to confess his sin. Others were influenced by his honesty, humility, and agony of soul. They also began to repent. One Korean church leader who had joined the missionaries came under such conviction that he went out and spoke to several hundred Koreans who had assembled, confessing his sin, and pleading for forgiveness.

Wave after wave of conviction, weeping, and repentance swept over the land, triggering a revival that affected tens of thousands and eventually millions throughout Korea. They became known in the mission world as The Praying Koreans. Mission workers from Korea are now serving in 175 counties, and it's second only to the US as a missions sending country. What happened was a big move of God, but it all began with one small act of repentance in response to God's revelation. A small act became a nation changer.

This book by my longtime friend and coworker Danny Lehmann is about the importance of taking small steps in obedience to God. This principle has deeply affected us in Youth With A Mission.

Back in 1973 I was on tour in Korea and quite excited about the acquisition of YWAM's first Mercy Ship. Early one morning after sleeping on the floor in an unfinished apartment, I awakened and saw in my mind's eye a picture of me standing before 300 YWAMers who were rejoicing over the big ship we believed God was releasing to us in New Zealand. As they were laughing and cheering, I glanced behind me and saw a figure in shadows. His head was bowed, and I knew it was Jesus. In that moment, I also realized we had exalted the ship over him. For the next two hours I wept in that empty apartment. I told the Lord, I didn't want the ship if it separated us from him.

Two days later I flew to Osaka, Japan, for YWAM leadership meetings where I began telling our leaders around the world what I'd seen. For the next few days we were on our faces weeping. Even small areas of sin were exposed. Things we saw as little were big in the eyes of God, and in this time of repentance we gave the ship back to the Lord. On the sixth day we sensed the Lord's forgiveness and approval. His presence was glorious, majestic.

Next I had to go on to Wellington, New Zealand, to speak to the ship crew about how God had humbled us and led us to give up the ship. They had been working long hours to prepare it, so this decision hit them hard. The ship had generated a lot of publicity in New Zealand, and soon we came under sharp criticism from some sources. My wife Darlene and I returned to New Zealand and toured the country for a few weeks, asking church leaders to forgive us for taking glory that belonged to Jesus.

I thought we had lost all credibility, but to my surprise I was invited to speak at Billy Graham's Lausanne Congress on World Evangelization a few weeks later. I explained to Dr. Graham's assistant what had just happened. He said, "Billy understands. It's just the working of God in your life." So I spoke about how God had humbled us. From then on more people began to invite us to tell our story. Multiplication began in YWAM – much bigger than we could have imagined.

Humility is being known for who you really are. This definition from the writings of Evangelist Charles Finney reflects on the amazing example of Jesus, who invites His disciples to "deny themselves and take up their cross and follow me…" (Mark 8:34). Our big God, creator of all things, came not in great power and glory but as a little baby with a questionable beginning. In the eyes of some, He was an illegitimate son, born to young girl in an animal shelter. God loves to begin big things in little ways.

There's a song that often plays in my mind. It says "little is big when God is in it." That's exactly what this book is about. It's author Danny Lehmann, whom I've known for decades, is one of my heroes. He's an evangelist among evangelists, a teacher among teachers, a leader among leaders. His books and radio ministry have inspired thousands. This book on little things will inspire you to do the small steps of obedience and leave the big things to God. Open your heart to God and see what adventure of faith He'll begin in your life.

Loren Cunningham
Founder of Youth With A Mission

INTRODUCTION

"For by the grace given me I say to everyone of you:
Do not think of yourself more highly than you ought,
but rather think of yourself with sober judgment…"
(Romans 12:3)

I spend a lot of time in airports. God has called me to serve Him in world missions and this requires travel. On one trip I had been invited to speak at a missions conference and was at the airport curbside waiting for someone from the local ministry to pick me up. As I waited, my thoughts went through this progression:

0 minutes – "Oh…no one is here. I'm sure they'll be here shortly."

5 minutes – "Maybe they're giving me a little extra time to get my bags."

15 minutes – "Hmmmm…maybe they got caught in traffic."

30 minutes – "I gave them my cell phone number, my assistant double checked it!!!"

40 minutes – "I should have rented my own car…this is a hassle."

After forty-five minutes, with my patience level exhausted, I found these now embarrassing words crossing my mind, "What's wrong with these people? Don't they know who I am?!" Almost immediately some other words came into my mind, words that I knew were the voice of the Lord: "No, Danny, I guess they don't know *who you are*. Why don't you tell us *who you are?!*" I immediately felt ashamed of my attitude as the hot breath of God's Spirit conveyed His displeasure. I was deeply convicted and did some instant repenting. One minute later my ride showed up!

Since that incident I have spent a lot of time thinking, reading, and talking with others about why we have a tendency to "cherish exaggerated ideas" of ourselves (Rom. 12:3, Phillips) From my discussions, I have found that like many others, I have a strange sense of entitlement, thinking that I actually deserve to be picked up promptly, have my computer work at an accepted speed, have people return my phone calls in a timely fashion and in general, expect the whole world to revolve around me. After all, it is all about me, isn't it?

One would think so. For as I write this, the top three best-selling books in the Christian non-fiction category of Amazon.com are also listed in the personal transformation, New Age, and self-help categories. Many authors and teachers pander to our desire to live in the false reality that life is indeed all about us. Regardless of how many Christian self-help books we read, there is only one way to the abundant life Jesus taught about and that involves dying to ourselves.

The little book you're holding is an attempt to diagnose the disease of pride and self-righteousness and to suggest a cure (humility and faithfulness). Start with a spiritual EKG (heart test), drink in a generous dose of God's Word, do a gut-level reality check, and absorb all the wisdom you can from those who have already traveled this road to wholeness.

This book is also written with the promise that there is an abundant, fulfilling, wonderful Christian life that puts a spring in your step and stokes your spirit. The Greek word *zoe*, describes a vibrant, fulfilled life. This is opposed to *bios*, mere existence. *Zoe* is not attained by seeking after an abundant life, but by simply cultivating the characteristics of what I have come to call the Next-Big-Thing lifestyle.

I considered several options when looking for a title for this endeavor: The Glory of the Mundane, The Excitement of the Ordinary, and even for a second considered The Rapture of Regulated Routines! I finally settled on the present title as most accurate to describe what I am trying to say. In over thirty-five years of walking with Jesus, observing the lives of hundreds of other Christians within my orbit, reading the stories of great saints of the past, and studying the Bible, I have come away with the following conclusion: The most successful Christians are the ones who get up every morning (preferably early), pursue some type of regular devotional surrender to God's will, seek a regular "fill up" with the Holy Spirit, roll up their sleeves and go out into God's world, and actually do something that is of value to His kingdom. As actor-director Woody Allen once said, "Ninety-five percent of success is showing up!"

So welcome to the journey into *The Next Big Thing*. As you read, keep in mind two guiding questions repeated in one way or another throughout the book: What was the last thing God told you to do – and did you do it? And, are you ready to do the Next Big Thing God tells you to do?

Danny Lehmann
Fall 2011

1

WHY "LITTLE" IS THE NEXT BIG THING

I'm a little guy – 5'6" if I really strrrrreeetch out. Being the shortest guy in my graduating classes at school and one of the smallest guys in my neighborhood created lots of self-image issues for me. I would be less than honest if I didn't admit that I felt a constant ambition to be big. As I grew older, I experimented with ways of compensating for my lack of stature – like talking big. Unfortunately, this did little to help me out of my feeling of littleness and got me into more than a few scrapes. I've got the scars and false teeth to prove it. Often either my own foot or someone else's fist would end up in my big mouth!

I dreamed of being a baseball, football, or basketball star, but I simply wasn't big enough. The few athletic endeavors I could do relatively well – running, surfing, and wrestling – didn't require a big body, but did require outstanding talent. I had neither. I spent my late teen years trying to be big at partying, drinking, and drug-taking. I once even made a half-hearted attempt at suicide. "I'll show her," I said to myself regarding the blonde who had recently dumped me. I climbed high up on a rooftop with the idea of jumping and making a big splat. But while I was up there, I had the distinct impression that I might get hurt! I sheepishly found my way down. The result of my search for "bigness?" There was a God-shaped empty place inside my heart. Then, I met Jesus.

Wonderfully transformed by the power of God, I realized that God accepted me just as I was: big or little. I also was exposed to healthy Bible teaching that made it clear to me that God was pleased more by small steps of faith than by any big religious performance. As I went through drug rehab and some basic discipleship, my walk with the Lord began to grow. After I began serving in ministry, I quickly was elevated into leadership, the speed of which was not so unusual during the 1960s Jesus Movement.[1]

Being a wide-eyed "new kid on the block," I looked around for spiritual fathers – humble mentors and examples of a Christ-like life. To say I was disappointed would be an understatement. It seemed much of the Christian leadership I observed displayed the same scamming,

---

[1] A spiritual awakening among counter-cultural youth in the 1970s, when thousands of western youths were saved and delivered from alcohol and the occult.

backroom maneuvering, and elbowing for position that I saw out in the world before I came to Christ. Fortunately, God had instilled in me a hunger for His Word, and I saw in Jesus the model I was seeking. I devoured the Bible, especially the life and words of Jesus.

My understanding of big and little ran into a buzz saw when confronted with Jesus' example and teaching. They seemed to be constantly pointing *down* as opposed to *up* the ladder of success and stature. He came *down* from Heaven, bowed *down* to wash His disciples' feet and "made himself nothing, taking the very nature of a servant" (Phil. 2:7). Finally, Jesus went as low as you can go – to the Cross. He indicated that His kingdom was made up of people who understood that the least would really

> *My understanding of big and little ran into a buzz saw when confronted with Jesus' example and teaching.*

be the greatest and that in our weakness we would be made strong, in humbling ourselves we would be exalted, in making ourselves poor we would thereby become rich, and in dying to ourselves we would live. Hmmmmm! My worlds were colliding!

Thankfully, I met other leaders who were truly humble and were content with little, as far as their standing among men. I joined Youth With A Mission (YWAM) primarily because of the example I saw in two YWAM leaders, Kalafi Moala and David Hall. While on an outreach to Fiji, I observed them serving in humble ways without seeking attention. These men had a big vision to evangelize the world, but were able to balance those big dreams with egos very much under control. This contrasted sharply with examples of selfish ambition I had earlier observed.

Another thing that helped me come closer to lining up with a God's view of big and little was a season when I camped in the first chapter of Philippians. Paul asked God to help the believers to "abound in insight and discern what was best." The literal words in the Greek are translated "… put to the test things that differ…" In other words, having love as a foundation and spiritual discernment as their guide, they were to put to the test anything that "differs" from God's perfect plan and thereby "approve what is excellent" (Phil. 1:10, KJV). Paul began the letter building up their confidence that God would complete what He'd started in them (v. 6). Then after praying for them, he made reference to those who, though genuine gospel preachers, had mixed motives underlying their ministry (vv. 15-18). He wanted to protect them from this mixture and get them focused on the "excellent."

As I meditated on this Scripture, its timeless truths became a "discerner of the thoughts and intents of the heart" (Heb. 4:12, KJV). I began to sense a sort of divine spotlight on my heart – and what it revealed wasn't pretty. I was growing as a Christian leader, but my motives were far from excellent.

God showed me that some things I did in His service were not just a gray mixture of Spirit and self, but down-right black – a color which was an apt metaphor to describe my selfish heart. God showed me what He had revealed to the prophet Jeremiah 2,600 years before, that my heart was "deceitful above all things, and desperately wicked" (Jer.17:9, KJV). And, like Jeremiah, I had a difficult time even knowing my own heart until it was put to the test. When God aimed His light into the dark caverns of my soul, I was shocked.

When God aimed His light into the dark caverns of my soul, I was shocked.

Pride is deceptive by nature (Obad. 1:3). This was why Jeremiah said, regarding his heart, ". . .Who can understand it?" (Jer. 17:9). God, in His mercy, sometimes allows us to probe the hidden places of the soul so He can help us "discern what is best" (Phil. 1:10). God opposes the proud (1 Peter 5:5) and wants to expose our arrogance, self-centeredness and pride and help us walk in humility. The problem is, we can't see our pride because of its self-deceptive nature and hence we are unable to know our own hearts.

The answer? We need to be broken. If I were sitting with you face-to-face, and asked, "Do you have pride in your life? Are your motives for serving God mixed choices that make you look big?"--what would you say? If you are like most people, you would shrug your shoulders, hoist the white flag of surrender and say something like, "Sure, I guess. But doesn't everybody? I...I...mean, nobody's perfect!" If again, you are like most people it wouldn't "hit" you unless God, by His Spirit, was doing the hitting.

Once, early in my spiritual journey, I had such a hit. Cheryl, a friend, asked to have a word with me. "Danny, when I first came to town, you were this surfer guy who was on fire for God, full of the joy of the Lord, the fruit of the Spirit, and a zealous soul winner. But something has changed, bro'. You've become negative, critical, angry, and if you don't mind the word – *religious*. Before, you were an example of a happy, carefree, childlike, contagious Christian. And now... well...you're different... we want the old Danny back!" Somehow without my realizing it, in my pursuit of God, I had morphed into a modern-day Pharisee with a lot of religious trappings and not much life.

Although at first I was defensive, soon the Holy Spirit used Cheryl's words to penetrate my proud heart and I repented. It was then that I was introduced to Roy Hession's book, *The Calvary Road.* I read the first chapter – "Brokenness" – six times. I found myself in an eerily similar place as the author. Hession, as a successful young evangelist in England found he was "dry" because he was "high" on himself. He wrote that he needed to be broken to truly experience revival and allow God's living water to flow in his soul. Likewise I had devel-

Being very aware of all the things I was doing for God… I noticed that others were doing much less…

oped an inflated estimation of myself and was in need of a similar breaking.

My pride came from the belief that I knew the Bible better, attended more meetings, and witnessed more than most of my friends. I was also big on the "don'ts" – no movies, TV, alcohol, etc. Being very aware of all the things I was doing for God (unbroken people usually are!), I noticed that others were doing much less (unbroken people usually do!), and I esteemed myself more highly than I should (Rom. 12:3). Cheryl and Roy Hession loved me enough to point it out. Shortly thereafter, the joy and the fruit returned and I once again began to follow Paul's advice to "approve the things that are excellent" (Phil. 1:10, KJV).

Fast forward twenty-five years. I was serving on YWAM's Global Leadership Team and fifty of us were meeting near London for our annual strategy conference. My wife stayed home in Hawaii to care for her aged mom who had recently suffered brain injury from an aneurism. One day, I called home to check in on Linda and ask how she was doing. As the conversation went on, she asked me about our meetings. Without consciously trying to sound big, I told her how we were developing strategies for mass evangelism and penetrating unreached people groups with church planters. I was making plans to get my books published in different languages and making projections as to how we could multiply our training schools worldwide and complete the Great Commission. I was also involved in the initial phases of the "Call 2 All" movement.

I suddenly realized that the whole conversation was revolving around me. So I asked, "What have you been doing?" She explained that she had been, among other things, "Helping my mother go to the toilet and experiencing the presence of the Lord!" As my jaw dropped on the other end of the line, it hit me that what I was doing might not have been so big after all!

What's the Big Idea?

That is how this book was born. Just as in the contrast of big missionary planning (not that there's anything wrong with that) and little service to an elderly woman, this book is about contrasts. It recognizes that we are all surrounded by big ideas that seductively entice us to join the quest for bigness. Our world constantly exposes us to and promotes the concept of big: entrepreneurs who build big companies, professional athletes who secure big contracts, body builders who build bigger bodies, and people who can land a lot of publicity on network television simply because they have big egos and are famous for being famous. All "bigness," however, is temporary.

But before we get too pompous in criticizing the world's upside-down value system, those of us who claim to follow Christ should ask where we are on the big/little quadrant. For instance, do we sometimes find ourselves in awe of Christian "stars," impressed with leaders of mega-churches and preachers with "big" ministries? As an author I have to deal with a jealous heart toward authors like Rick Warren and Max Lucado who sell, literally, millions more books than I do! And why am I jealous? It's simple. It's because I want to be big like them. But we have to ask ourselves, "Where is Jesus in all this?" What is motivating this incessant pursuit of big, even as we follow the One who gave up all things big to rescue us from the futility of this endless pursuit of bigness.

Jesus is God. You can't get much higher than that and yet He was crucified as a common criminal. You can't get any lower than that. I would like to suggest that what we consider big, even in the Christian world, is not necessarily big from God's point of view. Some of this is painfully self-evident. We can see that big success in Christian ministry is not always matched by big character. One evangelist friend of mine sarcastically sniped, "I have been involved with big men of God who were big bozos!"

A few years ago I received a brochure in the mail advertising an upcoming Bible Conference. I couldn't help but notice the plethora of big-name, nationally-known speakers on the schedule. Then I noticed the photo of a guy alongside these speakers who was relatively unknown.

> *I would like to suggest that what we consider big, even in the Christian world, is not necessarily big from God's point of view.*

He just didn't seem to "fit" with the others. Then it hit me. He was the guy organizing the conference! I laughed out loud. "Sure, this 'little' guy is promoting himself to the level of the 'big' guys so we will all be impressed. What a phony!" I found I had appointed myself judge and jury of this fellow's motives. It was then that I heard that distinct, clear convicting voice from Heaven, "Danny, don't laugh. You would have done the same thing yourself!" I laughed out loud again as I nodded my head in agreement. It was as if Jesus and I were having a good belly-laugh together. My proud heart was once again exposed.

Recognizing a lot of selfish ambition in me and others has forced me back to my Bible and the life of Jesus for answers. I looked afresh at His references to little mustard seeds, the faith of little children, and the constant warnings He gave us about big money and big egos. I studied Apostles Peter, James, and Paul's warnings about selfish ambition. I also took note that Jesus didn't seem all that impressed with large crowds, but instead spent most of His time with a small number of disciples. He understood that this little investment would produce big results!

A while ago, I was invited to speak at a Call 2 All Missions Conference in Orlando, Florida. My wife and I checked into a hotel a few blocks from the conference venue. On my way back from one of the sessions, I purchased a bottle of orange juice from an Indian man who was looking after the small hotel convenience store. I opened the conversation by making the observation that he looked like he was from India but his name tag displayed a Portuguese name. I then asked him if he was from Goa. His face lit up and he asked me how I knew he was from Goa. I told him I had spent a lot of time in India and knew the profound influence the Portuguese had in settling the area around Goa.

Our friendship continued over the next six days as I dialogued with him about religion (he was a Hindu), politics, our families, and other subjects. Not being overly busy in the shop every day, he had time to read. He devoured all my gospel tracts as well as my book, *Stoked.* By the end of the week he and his entire family surrendered their lives to Jesus.

Ironically, the title of my message at the conference was "The Call to the One," highlighting personal evangelism. We were strategizing on the big picture of how to reach the unreached billions. But the Lord gave me a living metaphor of my message, by showing Linda and me His love for this little Indian man from Goa.

The Next Big Thing in your life and mine should be the next thing God tells us to do, whether it looks big or little in our eyes. The very fact that God tells you to do it makes it big! Our Next Big Thing is the next person God puts in front of us to love and to serve in His name. It is the next action He tells us to do, whether it be big or little in our own estimation. It is the next encouraging word we can speak to someone who needs to be built up, the next hug we can give to the lonely, the next act of mercy we can show to the poor, the next smile we can give to the depressed, the next prayer we pray, or next commandment we obey.

I have not always been so good at living the Next-Big-Thing-lifestyle. A few years ago a young man named JP visited our YWAM training base in Honolulu every week for our Friday night community meeting. He was severely handicapped due to an accident and confined to a wheelchair. It took every bit of his energy to eek out a sentence or two of nearly unintelligible words. Most of us took a few minutes every Friday to love on him and to make sure

The Next Big Thing in your life and mine should be the next thing God tells us to do, whether it looks big or little in our eyes.

he was comfortable during our worship and preaching times. One night I was a bit over-hyped (I have a type A personality!) and was in a hurry to get our students out on the streets witnessing after our meeting.

I saw JP out of the corner of my eye, but made the choice to NOT to engage him. I consciously avoided him so we could leave immediately to the outreach.

In the van on the way downtown, I was severely convicted by the Holy Spirit. It was as if He said, "The high point of JP's week is to visit you and the others there at the meeting. He is confined to the personal prison of his wheelchair twenty-four hours a day and you are so busy that you don't have five minutes to brighten his day." And then these words rang out in my heart: "If you have done it to one of the least of my brethren, you've done it unto me" (Matt. 25:40). I blew an opportunity to minister to Jesus in the parking lot that day. At that moment, I was too big to do the little thing. I missed my opportunity to do the Next Big Thing.

Even secular research is showing the importance of little, purposeful actions. Books such as *The Power of Small* by Linda Kaplan Thalor and Robin Koval, and *The Tipping Point – How Little Things Make a Big Difference,* and *Blink* by Malcolm Gladwell, give many illustrations and insights on why big successes, changes and social epidemics are started and "tipped" by little, sometimes split-second thoughts and actions.

John Wooden, the most successful basketball coach in college history, described in his autobiography an annual ritual in which he would show his new players how to put on their socks! "I wanted absolutely no folds, wrinkles or creases of any kind on the sock. Wrinkles and creases can cause blisters. Blisters interfere with performance during practices and games. These seemingly trivial matters, taken together and added to many, many other so-called trivial matters, build into something very big: namely your success."[2] Wooden believed that little things made the difference between champions and near-champions.

One of my missionary heroes, William Carey, said "Expect great things from God. Attempt great things for God." Sounds big, doesn't it? However, if you read about Carey's life, you will see that his continuous faithfulness in the small things led to the achievements that gave him the reputation as the father of modern missions. Once near the end of his life he was asked what factors contributed to his success. He humbly answered, "I can plod. I can persevere in any definite pursuit. To this I owe everything." Carey's metaphor of "plodding" is an apt description of the Christian life which is spoken of in the Bible 262 times as a "walk." Our faith destination is the result of many small steps that make up our journey. Enoch walked with God and thereby pleased Him – step by step (Gen. 5:24, Heb 11:5).

Does God want us to pursue big dreams? Yes. Does He want us to believe in and follow a BIG God? Yes. Does He want us to seek ever-increasing faith on our journey? Yes. Let's just do it God's way – one obedient step at a time.

---

[2]John R. Wooden, *They Call Me Coach* (New York: McGraw-Hill, 2004)

2

Big Things and Butterfly Wings

Joe came to see me one day looking very discouraged. He said he was breaking his commitment to serve as a staff member in our Discipleship Training School. When I asked why, he said: "I'm just dry. I don't feel God anymore. In my quiet times, I can't feel His presence and in worship times, I don't get excited about Jesus like the others. When I serve the Lord, it tends to be stale, routine, and religious. I thought when I got involved in missions that I could change the world. I thought I would accomplish something big, but now I can barely keep my own life straight. The Christian life used to be exciting, but now it has become a bore. I feel like I am not doing the students any good by continuing on with in my commitment. So, I'm going home."

Usually, when I hear something like this, I begin to fish around to find out if there is some hidden issue that is causing the dryness of soul. About an hour into the

21

conversation, after doing some sensitive listening to him as well as to the Holy Spirit, I concluded that there was no sin in his life and he didn't seem to be under satanic attack. After assuring him of God's love and our gratefulness for his service, I gave him a challenge.

"Where did you get the idea that God was somehow obligated to make your life exciting?" When he asked me what I meant by the question, I turned up the heat. I said, "It seems to me that you have gone to the King of the Universe and created certain hoops He needs to jump through. If He doesn't satisfy your expectations, then you are 'outta here.' You are in essence saying to God: 'I have come up with my own criteria as to what it means to experience Your presence. I need You to infuse me with a sufficient degree of excitement and feeling if I am to continue to be zealous for You.

Where did you get the idea that God was somehow obligated to make your life exciting?

"For instance, I really need You to 'show up' at least, say, sixty percent of the times I'm at worship with the feeling that You are inhabiting my praises. I also don't think it's unreasonable, Lord, for You to give me Your manifest presence in at least half of my quiet times and to pat me on the back with Your spiritual hand of satisfaction when

I do good work for You. Also on a semi-regular basis, I need You to help me feel wild at heart and live my best life now. I want to reap the benefits of the prayer of Jabez and have the assurance that I have a purpose-driven life!" In other words, I want to experience God!"

I made it clear to my young friend that I was not being critical of the books I had mentioned tongue in cheek. However, books like these tend to leave out "the rest of the story." Many like these are written with American presuppositions and read with American lenses, neither of which is necessarily biblical. I then probed deeper.

The Dark Night of the Soul

I had Joe open his Bible, and I showed him the following words: "Who among you fears the Lord and obeys the word of His servant? Let him who walks in the dark, who has no light, trust in the name of the Lord and rely on his God" (Isa. 50:10).

I explained that in the writings of the Apostle John, walking in darkness was equated with walking in sin and disobedience to the will of God. However, in this passage in Isaiah, God is commending the person as a God-fearing, obedient believer. He quickly adds, however, that this obedient, faithful servant was walking in darkness with no light. God then went on to warn him about walking in the light of his own fires.

This is the passage that Saint John of the Cross used as the basis for his classic book, *The Dark Night of the Soul*. Author-preacher A.W. Tozer called it, "the ministry of the night" while others made reference to the "winter of the heart" or the "ministry of absence." The point is that God Himself sometimes will withdraw the consciousness of His presence from us, take away the feelings of His nearness and cause us to walk in darkness for a while. How long that period lasts is up to Him. There is no mention in this passage about the Devil, sin or other reasons for the darkness. It is God Himself who is the cause. It is His way of adjusting the lenses of our big/little glasses and helping us focus on the "excellent."

My diagnosis of Joe's problem was that God was allowing him to walk in darkness so that he would learn to walk by faith and not by sight (see 2 Cor. 5:7). He wanted thereby to teach him not to doubt in the darkness what he had learned in the light.

> *He wanted thereby to teach him not to doubt in the darkness what he had learned in the light.*

The Scripture says that without faith it is impossible to please God, but that faith, by definition, is to be "certain of the things we cannot see" (Heb. 11:1, GNT). We are also told to "...fix our eyes not on what is seen, but on what is unseen, since what is seen is temporary but what is unseen is eternal" (2 Cor. 4:18). Joe was greatly encouraged that his "dryness" was actually a result of God's deep love and concern for him.

This walk of "unseen" faith is crucial if we desire the peace and security of a Next-Big- Thing lifestyle. We must trust God in the darkness. Obedience to the next thing God puts in our path cannot happen if we are not content in our present situation and are always on the lookout for something "big." Paul called this "the obedience that comes from faith" (Rom. 1:5, 16:26). German theologian and

Dietrich Bonhoeffer wrote... "Unless a man obeys, a man cannot believe."

martyr Dietrich Bonhoeffer wrote that "... the step of obedience must be taken before faith can be possible. Unless a man obeys, a man cannot believe."[1]

Years ago Campus Crusade President Dr. Bill Bright gave a simple illustration of a train with an engine, a coal car, and a caboose. The engine is called "Faith." The coal car called "Facts" represents the truth of God's Word,

---

[1] Dietrich Bonhoeffer, *The Cost of Discipleship* (New York: Touchstone Book, 1959), 66

which fuels the faith that keeps the train of our Christian life running. The caboose is "Feelings" which makes the train longer and perhaps more attractive, but is not necessary for the train to reach its destination. In other words, we need faith and facts, but we don't necessarily need feelings.

When we demand God's presence and don't appreciate His absence, we often succumb to an obsessive hunt for the next new "flavor of the month" Christian experience. And such experiences can actually function as a counterfeit for God's Next Big Thing. The hard-core reality is that spiritual highs or "words from heaven" are of little value until we actually do *something!* Salvation Army founder William Booth once said that what most Christians need is not a missionary call, but a kick in the pants!

> *Salvation Army founder William Booth once said that what most Christians need is not a missionary call, but a kick in the pants!*

We must remember that it is faith that overcomes the world, not feelings (1 John 5:4). This brings up an important point. If faith is unseen, then what does living by faith look like? Perhaps it's not always moving mountains and other big things. It is walking in simple obedience to a big God who also is in the little things – the hundreds of choices (Next Big Things) we make every day that contribute to a life of faith.

The Butterfly Effect

In 1961, scientist-philosopher Edward Lorenz was using an early-era computer to calculate a weather prediction when, as a shortcut on a number in the sequence, he entered the decimal 0.506 instead of entering the full 0.506127 in his calculation. The result was a completely different weather scenario. Lorenz's findings were published by the New York Academy of Sciences in 1963.[2] One meteorologist remarked that if Lorenz's chaos theory were correct, "one flap of a seagull's wings" could change the course of weather forever. In 1972, when Lorenz gave a speech to the American Association for the Advancement of Science and neglected to give a title to his speech, someone labeled his talk, "Does the Flap of a Butterfly's Wings in Brazil Set Off a Tornado in Texas?"

The scientific community later dubbed this concept the Butterfly Effect, describing it as "sensitive dependence on initial conditions in chaos theory."[3] I simply apply

---

[2] Wikipedia, Edward Lorenz, Butterfly Effect.
[3] Wikipedia, Chaos Theory, Edward Lorenz.

the Butterfly Effect by pointing out that little events and choices do have big consequences.

For instance, I recently watched a podcast of a pedestrian who stepped into a crosswalk when the light turned green. From the vantage of the traffic cam, I winced as I saw the unsuspecting fellow get run over by one of two cars which crashed into each other when one of them ran the red light. Miraculously, the man survived and I'm sure, lying in his hospital room, he had the "Why me?" question bouncing around in his mind.

> *I simply apply the Butterfly Effect by pointing out that little events and choices do have big consequences.*

If you were to deduce from simple cause and effect logic why those three individuals were in that intersection at that moment you would have to know every event that influenced their lives and their parents' lives back to the Garden of Eden! Why did the driver run the red light? He was drunk. Why was he drunk? He got in a fight with his wife. Why did he turn to alcohol when under pressure? He learned it from his father. Why did his father turn to drink? He was in the Vietnam War. Why was he in the war? He randomly received a low lottery number in the Selective Service draft. Why was there a Vietnam War?… This kind of cause-effect pursuit could drive you crazy! But we must admit, from a human point of view, it makes sense. Indeed, the reckless acts of one person affect millions.

For example, the horrible pain and suffering caused by HIV/AIDS has been traced back to a "Patient Zero of AIDS," the French-Canadian flight attendant named Gaetan Dugas.[4] Dugas claimed to have 2,500 sexual partners all over North America and was linked to forty of the earliest cases of AIDS in California and New York. Today there are thirty-three million people infected with AIDS worldwide in addition to fifteen million AIDS orphans (twelve million in Africa alone). Millions of others, such as the families and friends of AIDS victims, have broken hearts as a result of the Butterfly Effect originating with Patient Zero.

In his book *The Tipping Point,* author Malcolm Gladwell gives a positive illustration of the Butterfly Effect in New York City's rapid drop in crime in the 1990s. In 1965 there were 200,000 felonies a year in the city. By 1975 it was up to 690,000 where it stayed until it hit its peak in 1990. By the end of the decade, however, murders dropped by two-thirds and felonies were cut in half. On the subways violent crime was down seventy-five percent. What was up?

---

[4] Malcolm Gladwell, *The Tipping Point: How Little Things Can Make a Big Difference* (New York: Back Bay Books, 2002), 21

In 1985 the New York transit authority hired a criminologist named George Kelling as a consultant. He sold the authorities on the "Broken Windows" theory. Kelling and colleague James Q. Wilson argued that crime is the inevitable result of disorder. If a broken window is left unrepaired, people walking by will conclude that no one is in charge and that no one cares. Soon, other windows will be broken and the anarchy will spread to the streets, sending a signal that anything goes.

The Tipping Point describes how New York police were instructed to crack down on the "little" crimes such as fare evasion and graffiti on the subways (170,000 people a day were cheating at the subway turnstiles by jumping over them or jamming their way through at a cost of 150 million dollars a year). David Gunn, the new subway director, believed the graffiti was symbolic of the collapse of the whole system. As the cops busted the cheats and painted over the graffiti daily, they not only transformed the subway system, but saw the overall crime rate nearly cut in half. Little things make a big difference!

Several popular Hollywood movies have given us glimpses of the Butterfly Effect. In the Christmas classic, *It's a Wonderful Life* (1946), Clarence the angel, shows George Bailey (Jimmy Stewart) how rewriting history so that George was never born would affect the lives of everyone in his hometown in a negative way. In *Back to the Future II*, the Biff Tannen character gets his hands on a record book from 2015 and uses it to get rich. When the hero Marty McFly (Michael J. Fox) returns to his hometown in 1985, he finds it utterly degraded by the greedy Tannen. Other films like *Frequency* and *The Time Machine* have given us similar insights. With just a bit of imagination we can see how one twist of "fate" – a longer conversation, a traffic jam, stopping to tie one's shoelaces – can affect our whole life, and consequently the lives of others.

As believers in a sovereign God, however, we don't accept that our lives are in the hands of fate or chance. "My times are in your hands" (Ps. 31:15), but this doesn't necessarily mean that God meticulously controls every event in our lives. Biblical divine sovereignty allows for quadrillions of events to unfold and influence each other everyday. His sovereignty gives Him the

> *Biblical divine sovereignty allows for quadrillions of events to unfold and influence each other everyday. His sovereignty gives Him the authority to decide when to intervene.*

authority to decide when to intervene. That is where we come in. Our choices, prayers, and acts of obedience (little and big) are truly significant in God's plan. We can, as we are led by and obedient to His Spirit, make history.

Some, of course, have used Lorenz's Butterfly Effect and the questions raised by such reasoning to believe the Universe came together by a combination of time plus matter plus chance, and that there is no order, purpose, or meaning in anything. The famous atheist, Richard Dawkins, in his best-selling book, *The God Delusion*, used this seeming randomness as a key reason for his unbelief.

From a biblical worldview, however, we understand that God created the Cosmos as it is, and within it – from the smallest atom to the largest galaxy – there is an orderliness, complexity, and elegance that even hardened atheists and evolutionists often find difficult to explain. God certainly was not taken by surprise by the "mistake" that Lorenz made on his computer, which led to the Butterfly Effect concept. His infinitely intelligent and ordered mind understands chaos theory, but motivated by infinite love, He promises "that in all things God works for the good of those who love him, who have been called according to his purpose" (Rom. 8:28).

For years, Christian theologians and philosophers have sought to explain how God's divine sovereignty works together with our free choices. Some have taken the opposite approach to chaos theory and have said that God determines by His will *everything that happens*. This would include the most horrendous acts of violence, injustice, and other sins that God has declared explicitly in the Bible not to be His will!

At the opposite extreme are those who suggest that God is sometimes unpleasantly surprised by the selfish or senseless acts of His free creatures and is always playing catch up to respond to peoples' choices. I simply put up the white flag of surrender and plead "mystery," and I'm content with that. I suggest you do the same.

Looking at the Butterfly Effect in a more redemptive and simple way, I would like to suggest that God is in Heaven wanting His will to be done. He tells us to know, pray for and do His will (Matt. 6:10, Col. 1:9 & 4:12). He makes His will clear to us in the Bible and speaks to us by His Holy Spirit on a regular basis. As we are led by the Spirit of God, He invites us to do the Next Big Thing that is in front of us so that He can work His will out in the lives of His people and in the nations of the world. This is why divine guidance and seeking God in detail is no little thing. Our daily choices are significant in His plan. In other words, He's in the little things.

As we are led by the Spirit of God, He invites us to do the Next Big Thing that is in front of us so that He can work His will out...

Ananias and the Next Big Thing

Saul of Tarsus is found in the opening verse of Acts 9 "... still breathing out murderous threats against the Lord's disciples." Saul is *big* as a self-righteous Pharisee. God, who is bigger, knocks him down to size, speaks to him in an audible voice, and strikes him blind. For three days, God lets Paul think about the consequences of his persecution of the Christians and therefore of Christ Himself. Along comes a *little* disciple named Ananias. With the exception of Paul's testimony in Jerusalem we hear nothing of Ananias before or after this event. Ananias randomly shows up in the story and is commissioned by God to perform a simple task (Acts 9:10). God calls his name and he responds, "I am here, Lord." Here we find the beauty and simplicity of the person ready to do the Next Big Thing. He was simply "there." The NIV translates his response as "Yes, Lord." Ananias was the original "yes man!"

Author Chuck Swindoll describes some people as having a "yes face." They are grace-filled Christians who are there when you need a favor and who consider doing the Next Big Thing a privilege. Swindoll contrasts these folks with those who display a "no face." Even if they do perform what was asked of them, they usually do it with a bad attitude. We, like Ananias, should be "yes" men and women.

What God called Ananias to do seemed like a relatively little thing. He was to pray for Saul and then get back to his business. The rest is history. We can now observe the things that Paul the Apostle did in his life which have had a cumulative Butterfly Effect on millions of believers who have read his writings and followed his example. Ananias? He faded into obscurity, but it was his fifteen minutes of fame with the disillusioned Saul that changed history. He simply was obedient and faithful to do the Next Big Thing.

How do we apply this to our lives? It's a simple question of obedience linked with humility. God resists the proud (people who are focused on their own version of the Next Big Thing). When He wants to *promote* someone (Ps. 75:7-8), He looks for those who voluntarily pursue the little, the last, and the least.

> *God resists the proud (people who are focused on their own version of the Next Big Thing).*

One such person was Saul of the Old Testament. He was out searching for lost donkeys when the prophet Samuel came to anoint him as Israel's first king. Saul's response: "But am I not a Benjamite, from the smallest tribe of Israel, and is not my clan the least of all the clans of the tribe of Benjamin?" (1 Sam. 9:21). Yes, that is exactly the kind of person God is looking for. We know that Saul eventually turned *away* from God, but the anointing he received that day was real. God delights in using people who have humble opinions of themselves.

Too many believers today are like religious butterflies flitting from one conference, retreat, or spiritual happening to the next in search of something big. Prophets on the circuit regularly quench the thirst of these butterflies with the intoxicating nectar of (often counterfeit) predictions of big things to come. If they don't find it in this experience or that personality, these sincere, cross-pollinating seekers of the Next Big Thing will keep searching until their thirst for bigness has been met. Please don't misunderstand. I believe we should heed Paul's warning not to despise prophecy (1 Thes. 5:20), and there is nothing wrong with attending inspiring conferences with exciting speakers.

There must, however, come a time in the believer's life when Jesus is enough. We must also recognize that prophecy is intended to build us up, not puff us up! I find it interesting that the first prophecy Paul received was about how

> *We must also recognize that prophecy is intended to build us up, not puff us up!*

many things he was to suffer for his faith (Acts 9:16). I have seen *many* (especially young) believers that have their hopes and expectations built up only to be cast down when some would-be prophet's big predictions didn't come to pass. Then seeds of unbelief grow, and they begin to doubt whether God speaks to us at all. Believers need to develop discernment skills and learn to "Test everything. Hold on to the good" (1 Thes. 5:21). This warning immediately follows the command not to despise prophecy.

What if God brought a prophet to you who said, "The Lord wants you to know that He has chosen you for something special. He has called you to labor in obscurity in the Amazon, attacked daily by mosquitoes in the jungle and slanderers on the Internet and, like Jesus, you will be condemned to die at a young age." Would this be okay with you? Is that BIG enough for you? Does God have to meet your criteria or definition of big? Is He serving you or are you serving Him?

Does God have to meet your criteria or definition of big? Is He serving you or are you serving Him?

One of my mentors, Pastor Chuck Smith, has been asked on many occasions how he pastors one of the largest churches in America and how he leads a movement that is now touching nations. He shrugs his shoulders and says, "I don't know. I've never done this before." He will often reflect back to a home Bible study when he was first given the oversight of Calvary Chapel Costa Mesa. His goal was to make that little handful of people the best biblically-trained believers in Orange County. He had no grandiose visions, no bold positive confessions. He has never written a book on how to grow a big movement. His bottom line: Be faithful and do the next thing God tells you to do.

My life was radically transformed one day when two guys approached me – a dazed and confused surfer mindlessly watching the waves – with a little gospel booklet. That tract cost a dime and took only little bit of time. God used that small seed to do something big in my life. Thousands who have benefited from my ministry are also affected because of that five-minute encounter with a ten-cent tract.

How I thank God for the faithfulness of Kevin and Kelly White who approached me on the beach that day. They could have chosen to do a thousand other things, but they did the Next Big Thing which was to give a gospel tract to a spaced-out kid with long blond hair who was going nowhere fast. The butterfly flapped its wings and a tornado happened in my heart. God blew away all my sin, the guilt and the effects of four years of drug abuse, and a lifetime of insecurity about being a "little" guy. He gave meaning and purpose to my life. And by His grace, God has helped me influence many others.

Perhaps you will be influenced by this book and the Butterfly Effect will continue to help you to make an impact in the lives of others all over the world. I'm often asked by young people, "How can I make a difference in my world?" and "How can I really live an exciting Christian life?" My answer, "Do the next thing God puts in front of you, whether you consider it little or big. The next thing is the Next Big Thing."

3

LITTLE WORDS AND BIG THINGS

"For out of the overflow of the heart the mouth speaks. The good man brings good things out of the good stored up in him, the evil man brings evil things out of the evil stored up in him. But I tell you that men will have to give account on the day of judgment for every careless word they have spoken. For by your words you will be acquitted, and by your words you will be condemned."   – (Matt. 12:33-37)

In my opinion, the above passage is one of the most neglected of all the teachings of Jesus. Why? Because it's just so hard to swallow. Do we really believe that our words reflect what's in our heart? Do bad words equal a bad heart and good words equal a good heart? Furthermore, do we really believe we will give an accounting at God's judgment seat for "every careless word" we speak in this life?

If we truly want a Next-Big-Thing lifestyle, the heart/mouth connection is a big first step. Romans 10:10 says,

"For it is with your heart that you believe and are justified, and it is with your mouth that you profess your faith and are saved." Likewise 2 Corinthians 4:13 says, "It is written: 'I believed; therefore I have spoken. Since we have that same spirit of faith, we also believe and therefore speak...'" If you don't believe, your words will reveal it. Jesus plainly told the Pharisees that their words exposed what was in their hearts (Matt. 15:10-20).

The word "heart" in the Bible refers to the deepest part of our being, that which defines who we really are. From a spiritual standpoint, the heart drives all our most important life choices. So if the condition of our heart is our top priority and words are the outflow of our hearts, then keeping a tight reign (Jas. 1:26) on our tongue is crucial. Solomon put it this way, "Above all else, guard your heart, for everything you do flows from it" (Prov. 4:23).

> *If you don't believe, your words will reveal it. Jesus plainly told the Pharisees that their words exposed what was in their hearts.*

Returning to our big/little contrasts, the book of James gives us a few interesting metaphors to describe our words. He likened the tongue to a bit in a horse's mouth, a rudder on a ship, or a little match that starts a big fire. In the middle of his tirade against careless words, James declares, "Likewise, the tongue is a small part of the body, but it makes great boasts" (Jas. 3:5).

It has been pointed out that for every word in Hitler's book, *Mein Kampf,* 125 lives were lost in World War II, all from the destructive words of one little man who barely stood 5'9" tall! How many times have you been "burned" by someone's careless words? When we think about past gossip, slander, false accusations, rumors, and other "myth-communications" about us, some of us physically wince at the memory. But do you feel the same amount of pain when you think of times when you hurt someone else through slander, gossip and back-biting accusations? Probably not, unless God has exposed what's in your heart.

One of the most intense encounters I ever had with the Holy Spirit was at a Bible conference. I just happened to be seated next to the leader of another ministry that I had publicly criticized. We both listened politely to the message. At the end, the speaker invited everyone to get in small groups and pray for one another.

As soon as I turned to pray with my fellow leader, I immediately began to tear up and then break into full blown convulsive wailing. I then fell at his feet and asked him to forgive me for publicly criticizing him. The Bible tells us that, "The tongue has the power of Life and Death…" (Prov. 18:21). I had truly ministered death with my tongue to this brother, but was not sufficiently convicted until that moment. The Holy Spirit, like a laser beam zeroed in on all of my critical attitudes and proud spirit. My crying continued for about fifteen minutes, and I could hear whisperings of people who were concerned that I might be having some sort of breakdown. I was, but in a good way. I was broken by God who revealed the power of my words to assassinate someone else's reputation, and my victim was seated right next to me!

> *I was broken by God who revealed the power of my words to assassinate someone else's reputation...*

When the brother assured me several times of his forgiveness and said it was "no big deal," I raged in protest. "It **is** a big deal. It's a big deal to God and it's a big deal to me." I had used what the Puritans called the "sacred desk," set aside for the proclamation of God's Word, but turned it to a bully pulpit to slander this man's character in front of hundreds of people. I prayed for God's mercy and forgiveness.

I returned home emotionally exhausted that night. As I walked through the door, my wife Linda said, "What happened to you? It looks like you just got in a fight!" I said, "I did, with God – and He won!" I told her about the conviction of sin that God was laying on my soul. I went on to say, "Tomorrow I will write a letter of resignation from all my leadership responsibilities. I don't feel I'm to continue in ministry. I have decided to go back to construction work. In fact, I don't even know if I am saved and don't know if I ever was!" In characteristic wisdom, my wife didn't argue with me, but simply said, "Honey, I think you should get some sleep."

The next morning I woke up and took my customary prayer walk. Then the Holy Spirit spoke to me clearly and assured me that He still loved me, that I was not to resign my position, and that I was indeed saved as I had been since the day I accepted Christ. In conclusion, His word to me was, "I just wanted to show you your heart."

God had exposed hidden pride in my heart by the repulsive ugliness of my words. What made my sin so much worse was that I had been called to proclaim the good news about a God who sent His Son to earth to receive the judgment that was due to us. God had suspended His judgment on me at the cross, and what was my response – to jump out of the witness stand and into the judge's seat and render my own unrighteous judgment on someone else.

The Apostle James warned us about the double standard in our hearts that is exposed by our words when he said, "...no man can tame the tongue. It is a restless evil, full of deadly poison. With the tongue we praise our Lord and Father and with it we curse men, who have been made in God's likeness. Out of the same mouth comes praise and cursing. My brothers, this should not be" (Jas. 3:8-10).

After the above warning about its "poison," he switches metaphors and makes a few observations from nature: "Can both fresh water and salt water flow from the same spring? My brothers, can a fig tree bear olives, or a grapevine bear figs? Neither can a salt spring produce fresh water" (Jas. 3:11-12).

Jesus also used trees as a word picture for the connection between the heart and the tongue (Matt. 12:33-37) and made the same point as James: nature produces after its own kind. Where there is a fruit there is a root. Clean up your heart. How? Begin by choosing to honor God with your speech.

King David prayed that both "...the words of [his] mouth and the meditations of [his] heart..." would be pleasing to God (Ps. 19:14), and that he would have an "undivided" heart (Ps. 86:11). Likewise, Paul admitted to an intense internal battle between the good and evil in his own heart, and he cried out for the freedom to walk in the Spirit (Rom. 8:14-20). Returning to the imagery of our heart as a "spring," how can we maintain a consistent flow of fresh water untainted by the salt water of sin and self? I suggest you consider the discipline of "moving in the opposite spirit."

YWAM founder Loren Cunningham teaches a practice of simply choosing to move in the opposite direction of any temptation that assails us. For instance, as Jesus said, if someone smacks you on the right cheek, rather than punching him back, we should turn the other cheek. When we feel like someone is trying to rip us off, we are to respond to greed with generosity. When someone comes to us in hate, we are to respond in love (Matt. 5:38-45). Paul put it this way, "Do not be overcome by evil but overcome evil with good" (Rom. 12:21). This godly response has a curious boomerang effect and brings the blessing of God as we obey Him: "Cast your bread upon the waters, for after many days you will find it again" (Eccl. 11:1). One of the ways to obey

> *One of the ways to obey James' instruction to put a tight reign on our tongue is to minister in the opposite spirit with our words.*

James' instruction to put a tight reign on our tongue is to minister in the opposite spirit with our words.

Like a spring, "the words of a man's mouth are deep waters, but the fountain of wisdom is a bubbling brook"

(Prov. 18:4). Solomon adds, "the mouth of the righteous is a fountain of life..." (Prov. 10:11).

By contrast, "the wicked are like the tossing sea, which cannot rest, whose waves cast up mire and mud" (Isa. 57:20). What kind of water is springing forth from your mouth in the form of your words? Is it living water that brings life and health to those who listen? Or is it "mire and mud" gurgling up from a heart lacking both self-control and the fear of the Lord?

Like these various biblical metaphors express, our words can bring either life or death. May the Next Big Thing we do and the next big word we say express the beauty of Solomon's proverb, "a word aptly spoken is like apples of gold in settings of silver" (Prov. 25:11).

Positive Gossip

My wife, Linda, has a genuine gift of encouragement. One of the things she is fond of doing is spreading what she calls "positive gossip." She regularly talks about people to other people, but always in a good way and with a motive of building up those being talked about. It is the opposite of gossip.

For instance, we once picked up our friend Bob Fitts at the Honolulu airport. Bob is a humble, self-effacing kind of a guy and an anointed worship leader. Bob had just flown in from California, and he told us about the wonderful time he had leading worship at Harvest Christian Fellowship in Riverside CA, a church pastored by our mutual friend, Greg Laurie.

A few weeks later, we happened to be at a Bible conference with Greg. In casual conversation, Linda mentioned our airport ride with Bob from a few weeks before. She said, "Bob was telling us what a great time he had at your fellowship there in Riverside. He said your people treated him with such love and kindness and that your congregation really responded to his leading worship. Bob said he would love to come back there again. He called it one of the highlights of his year." Greg, looking a bit surprised, said, "Really? I was gone when Bob was at Harvest, but heard really good reports of his time at HCF. Some of our younger worship leaders were so impressed with how Bob led people into the presence of God."

Not long after this, we were in Kona having dinner with Bob and Kathy Fitts. Linda said, "Bob, we were just with Greg Laurie. Do you know what he said about you?" Bob looked a bit concerned and replied, "No. What?"

"He said he heard nothing but good things about your time there in Riverside and how some of his younger worship leaders were taking tips from you and appreciated you, and how he would love to have you back again to his church!" Bob said he would love to go back to Harvest and added that Greg was one of his favorite preachers.

Shortly thereafter, we randomly ran into Greg again and Linda "gossiped" about what Bob had said about Greg being one of his favorite preachers.

I have learned quite a bit from my wife about passing on positive comments. I also marvel at how she can pull something positive out of otherwise negative remarks. For example, if she's caught in a conversation in which negative things are being said about someone, she will pick the one positive out of the ten negative things that the critic said and spread that "gossip" on to the one being criti-

> *Jesus told us that the peacemakers would be blessed and one of the best ways to sow in peace is to sow little seeds of positive gossip all around the Body of Christ.*

cized. She purposefully neglects to pass on any of the nine potentially harmful things that were said. Jesus told us that the peacemakers would be blessed and one of the best ways to sow in peace is to sow little seeds of positive gossip all around the Body of Christ (Jas 3:17-18).

Another person who models this lifestyle of affirmation is my friend George Verwer. He is the founder of

Operation Mobilization, one of the largest missionary organizations in the world, with over 5,000 workers in eighty countries. He's also one of the most joyfully eccentric, crazy-in-love-with-Jesus guys you could ever meet.

A few years ago, George and I began our friendship by spending a week together. From then on, about every four months or so, I would receive a random phone call from George, from somewhere in the world he happened to be. I thought that was pretty special until I ran into Dave, a carpenter friend from Kauai who had grown up in Operation Mobilization. I discovered that George calls him too. A year later, Linda and I spent a day with Paul Eshelman, vice president of Campus Crusade for Christ International. We found out that George calls him too. I've since met several others who receive George's prayerful telephone calls.

On one trip together, I overheard George make calls to Christian leaders Franklin Graham and Gordon McDonald. Then he spent a long time talking to his wife's cousin. I thought to myself, "Who is this guy? He's on a first name basis with Billy Graham and runs a big missions organization, yet has time to make phone calls every month to scores of people. He adds value to international leaders, distant relatives, and obscure carpenters – all the while making spiritual life-giving deposits." Little things matter.

Judge's Seat or Witness Stand?

Like Linda and George, we have a choice to speak words that build up others or to be a conduit for destructive gossip and criticism. Because the Lord has chastened me about my proud heart and the subsequent use of harsh and critical words, I may be overly sensitive when I hear people criticize others. In fact, it is very hard for me not to be critical of critical people as I am about to do in this chapter! But somebody's got to do it, so hang on!

The Bible is full of warnings about the wrong use of words. There are boastful words, flattering words, exaggeration, murmuring, complaining, profanity, sexual jokes, lying, mockery, contention, slander, gossip, quarreling, perverse speech, angry words, verbal abuse, deceptive words, etc. The Word is clear about God's opinion about death-giving words. How is it that we tolerate such negative speech in our presence? Why don't we speak up, or at least refuse to listen to such soul-polluting talk? "Do not let any unwholesome talk come out of your mouths, but only what is helpful for building others up according to their needs, that it may benefit those who listen" (Eph. 4:29). The word "unwholesome" in this verse comes from a Greek word describing rotten, spoiling, smelly fruit! It may help to visualize walking into the living room of a friend's house with a garbage can full of putrid refuse and dumping it on your friend's new carpet. That's the picture this verse gives us of "unwholesome words."

The Internet has become a nesting ground for all kinds of ugly birds who love to pick and peck away at other people's reputations. In the days before cyberspace, a critical writer had to find some editor willing to publish their character attack. Today, however, everyone is fair game on the Web. Just Google anyone – from someone as prominent as Billy Graham to the latest evangelist who is beginning to make some impact for God, and you will find some caustic, hurtful and usually unsubstantiated criticism of that person. This is especially grievous in light of the Bible's clear warnings about criticism (Matt. 7:1-5, Rom. 2:1-4, 14:10, Jas. 4:11-12).

The word "unwholesome" in this verse comes from a Greek word describing rotten, spoiling, smelly fruit!

I make laps around the globe every year, traveling and meeting wonderful people from scores of different nations and denominations. I've met people from Bible churches, seeker churches, house churches, liturgical churches, emerging churches, "power" churches, denominational as well as non-denominational churches. I have had the privilege to drink from many streams that flow from the river of God (Ps. 46:4). I've found that the God of many-faceted grace (1 Pet. 4:10) has people represent Him in many different ways. But rather than recognizing and celebrating our diversity, the tendency in many churches is to think their viewpoint is the only accurate one.

Over time this hidden pride develops into an outwardly critical and self-righteous attitude that infects not only our hearts, but our words. Paul prayed for the divided Corinthians that they would have no divisions among them and that they would speak the same thing (1 Cor. 1:10). Unity and love for each other and *speaking as if we do* love each other are big priorities to God and should be to us as well.

> *Unity and love for each other and speaking as if we do love each other are big priorities to God and should be to us as well.*

Put simply, humility is sweet and pride stinks. Pride stinks in God's eyes and it stinks in the eyes of others. The only reason it doesn't stink in our own eyes is because we can't see it in all its hideous, repulsive ugliness. We are deceived by pride itself and by our own wicked hearts (Jer. 17:9, Obad. 3). We can, however, get a glimpse into what kind of root is in our heart by what fruit comes out of our mouths. How much ministry is fueled by self-aggrandizing platitudes designed for self-promotion? Only God knows.

Jesus said, "What is valued highly among men is detestable in God's sight" (Luke 16:15). I am convinced that our reputation in the eyes of non-Christians and whether or not we receive the fullness of God's grace will depend on whether or not we have the guts to admit that much of what we do is not for God, but for ourselves. We simply get big and little mixed up. We tend to prefer big because in all our pride we want to look good in the eyes of others. May we instead imitate John the Baptist who said, "He must become greater; I must become less" (John 3:30).

4

LEARNING TO LOVE WELL

"For whoever wants to save his life will lose it, but whoever loses his life for me will find it. What good will it be for a man if he gains the whole world, yet forfeits his soul? Or what can a man give in exchange for his soul?" – (Matt. 16:25-26)

In the above passage Jesus asks a rhetorical question about the value of a human soul, "What can a man give in exchange for his soul?" The answer is obvious – nothing. The previous question: "What good will it be for a man if he gains the whole world but forfeits his soul?" likewise has an obvious answer. It is of no value to gain the whole world and yet forfeit your soul. Conclusion: A human soul is worth more than all the material possessions in the world!

That truth was never clearer to me than during a time I visited Belo Horizonte, Brazil, a city of five million people with tremendous social needs. Under the leadership of

Johan and Jeannette Lukasse several fruitful ministries have been started in the city slums. One is a large house dedicated to caring for children infected with HIV/AIDS. In contrast to the chaotic, dirty urban sprawl outside, the inside of this house was immaculately clean, furnished simply, and organized with volunteers serving children from infants to seventeen years of age.

While visiting Refugio House, I asked about how the ministry was funded, the whereabouts of the children's parents, and the history of the ministry. I was particularly drawn to a young woman who was holding a slightly emaciated baby girl in her arms, rocking her back and forth like she was her own. She told me that most of the children were expected to die within days of their arrival at Refugio House. Many of them, however, lived for several years – astounding local medical professionals. As we discussed the gruesome reality that many of these children may never reach their teenage years, she replied with a pleasant smile, "We will keep little Pauola alive as long as we can, but until she dies she will know that God loves her and that we love her as well." It was an "aha" moment for me. Isn't that, in a nutshell, what life is all about – simply loving people well?

Jesus and the apostles described the Christian life in those same simple terms: *Love God and others* (Matt.

22:37-40, Jn. 13:34-35, 1 Cor. 13, 1 Pet. 1:22, 1 Jn. 4:8). Bible scholar Scot McKnight has bottom-lined this two-fold love command and called it *The Jesus Creed* in a book by that title. As we seek to do the Next Big Thing and love people well we must face the biblical tension between evangelism (saving souls for eternity) and social action (loving people today). That tension exists because Jesus not only gave us the Great Commission but also the Great Commandment and by His example modeled both.

Jesus said our love for Him is measured by our obedience to Him (Jn. 14:15). Hence, in His Great Commission He commanded us to make disciples of all the nations by teaching them to obey all His commands (Matt. 28:18-20). How do we obey *all* His commands? Especially, His command to love people well? I'd like to suggest three ways.

Loving People Well

Motivation #1 – Revelation: People Matter to God
First, we need to recognize that the eternal nature and value of a human "soul" is because all people are made in the image of God. Because of His infinite value, those made in His likeness are deserving of the same love afforded Him. The Bible writers called this love agape – the God-kind of love. God's love for us is not based on

performance, but value as His created beings. And since He created and loves all people, our love for people also should be impartial, as God's is.

Consider the parable of the Good Samaritan (Luke 10:30-37). Jesus' definition of who was our "neighbor" was the next person in His path who needed to be loved. The Jericho-bound robbery victim was the Samaritan's Next Big Thing. It was by design Jesus used a cross-cultural encounter in this story to illustrate His point: Love plays no favorites. He used the figure of a despised Samaritan to demonstrate to a man "from Jerusalem," that people matter to God – therefore we obey the Great Commandment.

Amy Carmichael, the legendary missionary to India, was once chastised by her superiors for doing too much social action. They were concerned that this was hindering her evangelistic impact in Dohnavur where she had established a home to rescue young girls from the prostitution industry. Her pithy reply: "You can't just pitch-fork souls into heaven. Unfortunately they are attached to bodies and you must deal with both."

You can't just pitch-fork souls into heaven. Unfortunately they are attached to bodies and you must deal with both.

A few years ago a church planter from North India named Anil felt prompted by God to move to Chennai, a city in the South. While prayer walking through the slums, he couldn't help but notice the horrible suffering of some of the 35,000 lepers dispersed among sixteen colonies in the city.

Their existence was a hell-on-earth. Treated as outcasts even from the lowest level of India's Hindu caste system, their days were spent begging in hopes of getting enough food to stay alive.

Although rejected by the lepers at first, Anil asked God what he could do. The Lord answered, "Open your eyes." Anil noticed at the end of the day's begging, these folks would hobble back to their make-shift colonies. With no feelings in their limbs it was extremely difficult to bandage their wounds or change the bandages. Anil did the Next Big Thing.

He showed up at dusk every evening, used a knife sterilized with medicated water to dig the stones out of their feet, washed their feet and applied fresh bandages for the next day's begging. When they ask him why he would do such a thing, when no one else would even visit much less touch them, he answered, "There is a God in heaven that wants to touch your heart, but first He wants me to touch your feet."

> *"There is a God in heaven that wants to touch your heart, but first He wants me to touch your feet."*

Today Anil has fifty-five workers on his staff consistently serving in the leper colonies, planting churches, and establishing training schools touching the untouchables, in the name of Jesus.

Motivation #2 – Imitation: What Did Jesus Do?

No one loved people like Jesus, and He is our ultimate role model. In His ministry He demonstrated by His actions that the kingdom of God was both present and future. Once, after delivering a demonized man, He declared, "…The kingdom of God has come to you" (Lk. 11:20). He spoke with equal passion about the eternal issues of heaven and hell as He did about loving people well in the here and the now. His plan for us is to be united with Him for eternity.

Shortly after declaring Himself to be "the resurrection and the life" and that His followers would never die, He wept and "groaned in His spirit" at Lazarus' grave (Jn. 11). Why? It wasn't simply because His friend died for Jesus certainly knew He would raise him from the dead. He wept because of the grief that death had brought to Lazarus' sisters and friends. Suffering and death make life so stinking hard and because Jesus is both God and man, He "gets it!" He displayed similar compassion when He saw the people as helpless sheep without a Shepherd

(Matt. 9:35-38). Jesus' response was a prayer for workers to love them well. Jesus embodied both the Great Commission and the Great Commandment.

Another way we can love people well is by obeying Jesus' command to seek His kingdom first. What did He mean by this? He couldn't have meant merely heaven. We know the kingdom will not come in its fullness until Jesus returns. We are to not only seek the kingdom, but pray for it, enter it, demonstrate it and live under its King's righteous rule in the here and the now (Matt. 6:10, 33, 18:3 and Rom. 14:17).

The fact that birds have two wings is an apt metaphor for the twin commands to love people well by both preaching the Gospel and demonstrating God's love. Historically the liberal wing of the church has flown in circles with the wing of social action and has consequently resembled little more than a Christian Peace Corps. Meanwhile, the conservative wing has flown in circles around the

Let's fly straight, seeking His kingdom first, proclaiming His words, doing His works, following His ways and giving His warnings…

future heavenly issues, often neglecting Jesus' prayer for God's kingdom to come "…on earth as it is in heaven" (Matt. 6:10).

As we eagerly await Jesus' return and the full establishing of His kingly rule, let's be busy occupying until He comes (Luke 19:13). Let's fly straight, seeking His kingdom first, proclaiming His words, doing His works, following His ways and giving His warnings until that glorious day when the kingdoms of this world become the kingdoms of our Lord and of His Christ (Rev. 11:15).

Motivation #3 – Dedication to the Kingdom

I dedicated this book to my dear friend Kevin Darrough who went to be with the Lord during its writing. Kevin and his wife Kim are powerful examples of the Next Big Thing lifestyle. In the early 1980s they were sent to Manila to evangelize and plant churches. They were unprepared for the shocking poverty they encountered there. Near their mission base, they saw malnourished babies, kids without parents and many people lacking the basic necessities of life. Among them was Rosalinda. At eighteen months of age she was little more than skin and bones. Her father had died of tuberculosis and her mother tried desperately to keep Rosalinda alive.

While they had no formal medical training, Kevin and Kim did what they could to get Rosalinda medical help, basic hygiene and a home where she could not only survive but thrive. Years passed, and they lost touch with

Rosalinda. Then at a meeting in another city, she came bounding up to Kevin and Kim - healthy, vibrant and full of the joy of the Lord! She thanked them for doing the Next Big Thing. They had excellent training in strategic church planting, but found that their most effective strategy was simply to love people well.

A similar story is that of Hakani, a five-year-old girl in the Suruwaha tribe in the Amazon region. The Suruwaha are one of over 200 indigenous tribes that inhabit this isolated and often primitive area of Brazil. Hakani was condemned to die because of a tribal custom requiring that any child born with a club foot, cleft palette, speech defect, or as a twin, be buried alive so that it would take its last breath underground. The tribe believed that in doing this, the spirit that caused the deformity would not affect the rest of the tribe. Hakani was buried alive but miraculously escaped and with the help of her older brother, fled the Suruwaha area. These two children lived in the jungle for the next three years surviving on plants, tree bark, bugs, and rain water. One day she happened upon some Brazilian Christians working among the tribes in the jungle. They brought Hakani to the city and provided basic medical care.

As with all stories of redemption, God found a worker who saw the value of Hakani's soul and who was willing to be a catalyst of God's love for her. Marcia and her husband Edson Suzuki have worked in the Amazon basin for over twenty years simply "loving well" the next person that God put in front of them. With some of their fellow workers, their presence has literally saved lives and helped indigenous cultures to survive. Their ministry has brought health, healing and salvation to many people in the Amazon basin. Hakani was not able to go back to her tribe for obvious reasons, so Marcia and Edson adopted her. Hakani's speech defect was healed and today she is a fifteen-year-old, happy with a wonderful life. The Suzuki family continues to serve with the love of Jesus, doing the Next Big Thing God brings across their path.

The books of Robertson McQuilkin, an eighty-five-year-old missionary statesman and strategist, bristle with concern for the nations of the world, particularly the unreached and the poor. He taught and proclaimed this message in many nations. But in 1990, Dr. McQuilkin resigned as president of Columbia Bible College to devote himself to caring for his wife Muriel who was afflicted with Alzheimer's disease. Why? Because he simply wanted to love the one person that God entrusted into his care, and he did so faithfully until she died in 2003. Like my wife Linda's mom, Dr. McQuilkin's wife wasn't very valuable to the world. She couldn't do anything, accomplish anything, or contribute to anyone else's well-being. But she was very valuable to God, and her husband reflected the Lord's character by demonstrating his unconditional love.

We must not conclude from these examples that little is better than big, any more than big is better than little. God does call people, like Dr. Bob Pierce to begin a World Vision and thereby minister to hundreds of thousands of the Rosalindas and Hakanis of our world. He does call Christian business entrepreneurs and ministry visionaries to believe God for massive amounts of money and man-power to make "big" changes in our world.

My point is not to devalue such efforts. It is, how-ever, meant to remind us that no matter how big or far-reaching our ministry becomes we must never lose the value of one human being in the eyes of God. I'll close this chapter with a quote from a man who dreamed "big" and has left as a legacy the largest missionary organization in the world – Campus Crusade for Christ. The late Dr. Bill Bright, who was responsible for more people hearing the Gospel of Jesus Christ than anyone in human history, said the following:

"It is a sad fact that a large percentage of pastors and evangelists do not witness personally. As a result, they lose not only power with God and man, but they fail to model for other Christians who are looking to them for an example of a Christ-like witness…Without a willingness to speak to individuals about the love and forgiveness of our wonderful Savior, I would have very little credibility in speaking to the crowds."[1]

A similar statement is expressed in Dr. Robert Coleman's classic book, *The Master Plan of Evangelism.* Coleman's main thesis is that while Jesus' mission was to accomplish something big – the evangelization of the whole world – His strategy was concentrated mainly on training the twelve. Following His own model of small seeds growing into big trees and a little yeast changing a big lump

> *…He banked on the principle that a few disciples who were loved well and trained well could change the whole world.*

of dough, He banked on the principle that a few disciples who were loved well and trained well could change the whole world.

As we seek to obey the Great Commission and the Great Commandment, we will most likely find that the Next Big Thing will have to do with loving the next person God brings across your path. Be careful never to lose sight of who's first priority in God's eyes. Many "successful"

[1] J.D. Douglas, *The Calling of an Evangelist, the Second International Conference for Itinerate Evangelists, Amsterdam, The Netherlands* (Minneapolis: Worldwide Publications, 1987), 27

men and women of God have tasted the success of ministry and at the same time lost the value of people.

Dr. Bright's Jesus film has had four billion viewings. His tract, the "Four Spiritual Laws," has been printed over three billion times. But in all his success he never lost his vision for the value of a human soul. Let's always remember that people matter to God.

5

IT'S A WONDERFUL LIFE!

"Lord, you have assigned me my portion and my cup,
you have made my lot secure. The boundary lines
have fallen for me in pleasant places. Surely I have a
delightful inheritance." – (Psalm 16:5-6)

"God loves you and has a wonderful plan for your life." So begins the most widely distributed Gospel tract in history. The simple message outlined in the "Four Spiritual Laws" has been used by the Lord to win millions of people to Christ and has been distributed in over ninety languages. In Chapter Two we made reference to the classic Christmas movie, *It's a Wonderful Life*. This brings up a question. Is there a "wonderful life" for us, full of supernatural evidence that a living God is the source of that life? Or is this simply an American appendage to the faith, a not-too-distant cousin of the Prosperity Gospel?

While some people take issue with reducing God's plan into such a simple, seemingly trite phrase, I think this is just what Jesus had in mind when He announced He came to give us "abundant" life or "life to the full" (Jn. 10:10). While not all Christians experience the same degree of personal peace and prosperity, when viewed from God's perspective, His plan is always wonderful. Why? Because we serve a wonderful God! He said to us through the prophet Jeremiah, "For I know the plans I have for you… plans to prosper you and not to harm you, plans to give you hope and a future" (Jer. 29:11).

Our Lot in Life

Psalm 16 is a prayer that begins with David asking God to keep him safe from danger. He could have complained about his not-so-wonderful life! However, in Psalm 16:5,6 he is in essence proclaiming: "Life is good. I am living the dream." He alludes to the imagery of the Old Testament boundary lines that were given when the tribes divided up the Promised Land according to Moses' decree (Josh. 13-21). The Levites (the tribe of priests) were not given a portion of land because the Lord was their inheritance. David, though not from the tribe of Levi, still proclaimed that the inheritance he had received from the Lord was "delightful" (v. 6).

Looking around at his difficult circumstances, David simply said he was content with his assignment from God, consisting of his portion and his cup, and that he considered his lot "secure" (v. 5). David said the boundary lines given to him had fallen in "pleasant places." He recognized that, along with his talents and treasures, God had given him boundary lines to keep him from being concerned about that which was not

David was grateful for what was given him by grace. What was not given by grace didn't concern him.

his concern. In other words, he experienced a wonderful life because he saw life through the eyes of God's grace. David was grateful for what was given him by grace. What was not given by grace didn't concern him.

One of the keys to living the dream is living under grace. God's grace is His favor. Just like Jesus described in the Parable of the Talents (Matt. 25), God chooses when and how much of His favor He gives to someone. Much of our frustration, religious striving, and unhappiness are rooted in discontent over the boundary lines of the grace that, God has portioned out for us.

This was the main roadblock to the Jews receiving God's abundant life. Jesus said to them, "How can you believe if you accept praise from one another yet make no effort to obtain the praise that comes from the only God?" (John 5:44). Later John added, "...they loved praise from men more than praise from God" (John 12:43). They were not content with what God had given them. Their boundary lines, in their estimation, had not fallen in pleasant places. They wanted more.

If there is a key to the wonderful life, it is this: That we seek God's favor alone and be content with what He, by His grace, gives us. I am an evangelist by God's grace. My friend Greg Laurie is also an evangelist by that same grace. By all measurements, Greg's evangelistic ministry is bigger than mine. He holds bigger meetings, sells more books, pastors a big church and influences far more people than I do. To the extent that I am jealous of or compare myself to Greg's ministry, I will rob myself of God's grace to live this abundant life. I will constantly push the boundary lines that God has given me. And as long as I keep pushing, I will not be a happy camper. Paul warned that those who compare themselves to others "...are not wise" (2 Cor. 10:12).

Paul was an apostle to the Gentiles "...by the gift of God's grace..." (Eph. 3:7). He said in another place, "I am what I am by the grace of God..." (1 Cor. 15:10). Later he described being under attack from a "messenger of Satan." He even saw this as a gift by God's grace to keep him from becoming proud because of powerful revelations he had received from God. He knew that the temptation to push the boundary lines of God's grace was great, so he was not only content at such trials but rejoiced when they came (2 Cor. 12:7-10).

Boundary lines are good. As poet Robert Frost wisely observed, "Good fences make good neighbors." Likewise, the choice to say, "The boundary lines have fallen for me in pleasant places" and to stay within those boundary lines makes a happy, contented Christian. Author-philosopher G.K. Chesterton once said, "Before you tear down fences you had better find out why they were put up." God's fences are not limits to, but protectors of His wonderful plan for our lives. This is just one of the many reasons His grace is amazing!

Your *Kuleana*

In ancient Hawaii, most land was owned by the *Ali'i*, the tribal chieftains. After the arrival of the missionaries and the subsequent conversion of some of the rulers, a more equitable division of wealth was decided upon. The Great Mahele land division of 1848 and the Kuleana Act of 1850 apportioned small plots of land "between the mountains and the sea" to the commoners. This *kuleana* was apportioned for them to cultivate and keep within their family. Unfortunately, corrupt Western opportunists soon took the land back from the Hawaiians. Nonetheless, it was, at least originally, an attempt to do right by everyone.

In modern Hawaiian, the word *kuleana* has evolved to refer to a sense of one's personal responsibility, in other words, our "lot in life." Our lives, comprised of the time, talents and treasures that God has given us to be stewards over, are in a sense our *kuleana*. We have our "lot" to cultivate and multiply its fruitfulness. Along with the stewardship over our *kuleana,* must come recognition of clear boundary lines that God has given as our *kuleana*. Not being content with our own *kuleana,* will continually rob us of the Lord's joy.

The life of Jonathan illustrates this aspect of the Next-Big-Thing lifestyle. Because of circumstances out of his control, Jonathan was rejected from being Israel's next King in favor of David. There was nothing in Israel that was "bigger" than being King! It would have been understandable if Jonathan wallowed in self-pity or rose up in anger at either his father Saul, his friend David, or with God himself.

Instead Jonathan lived out the principle of the Next-Big-Thing lifestyle. While 600 other warriors slept beside him, Jonathan decided to seize this next divine moment and do whatever he could for the glory of God. With the holy audacity of youth and a powerful faith in God (1 Sam. 14:2-6), he and his armor-bearer picked a fight with God's enemies. That day God gave him a great victory over the army of the Philistines. God only knows what the history of Israel would look like without Jonathan's obedience. He could have retreated in bitterness but he advanced as God moved him. Jonathan's lot was secure. His boundary lines were okay with him. Being the next king of Israel was not his *kuleana*. He was content to do the Next Big Thing.

I find it interesting that the one time David neglected his *kuleana* – staying at the palace while his men went out to war – he got into deep trouble by lusting after a married woman, another man's *kuleana*. As we observe King David's life we see, especially in the Psalms, that he experienced the absence as well as the presence of God. He had good days and bad days like everyone else. He sometimes complained to God about wicked people getting the goodies in this life while those who were godly got the crumbs. However, in Psalm 16 he said in essence: "I'm happy with where God has put me and it's all good." His personal mission statement contains three crucial ingredients to living the wonderful life.

1. **Peace in the present** ("I will praise the Lord who counsels me...because he is at my right hand I will not be shaken" (vs. 7- 8).

2. **Hope for the future** ("...you will not abandon me to the grave, nor will you let your Holy One see decay" (vs. 10).

3. **Joy for the journey** ("Therefore my heart is glad and my tongue rejoices...you have made known to me the path of life; you will fill me with joy in your presence, with eternal pleasures at your right hand" (vs. 9-11).

One of the things that has helped me experience more of God's abundant life is to pursue what author John Piper has called, "Christian Hedonism." Hedonism means to pursue personal pleasure. Most Christians would immediately reject such a pursuit as selfish and sinful. However, Piper points out that if our happiness is in God then we can truly find pleasure in God even if our lot in life has fallen on hard times. Piper's well-known dictum has become a sort of twenty-first Century beatitude: "God is most glorified when we are most satisfied in Him." Because of God's promise that joy is found in His presence (Ps. 16:11), abiding in Christ is the way to enjoy the abundant life. This is truly living the dream!

The Westminster Confession says it well: "The chief end of man is to glorify God and to enjoy him forever."

Small Steps to Spirituality

One sure way to enjoying the Lord, learning from Him, and growing in faith and obedience is to develop a daily discipline of prayer, study, and worship. Depending on your current devotional habits that may seem like too big a thing. But every journey is a series of small steps.

I learned a good lesson about small steps of spiritual growth from an example in Japan. After World War II, American occupation forces brought in experts to help with the rebuilding of Japanese industry. They introduced a concept centered on continuous improvement of work quality called *kaizen,* which became a key in the nation's competitive success. The goal was to set your goal a little higher every day and over months, those small improvements become big. If we could apply the *kaizen* philosophy to our daily routines, it could revolutionize our lives. Many musicians already do this. They know that adding five minutes of practice a day adds up to over thirty-six hours a year of self-improvement! Improving one percent per day adds up to 100 percent per 100 days.

Applying the concept of *kaizen* to our devotional lives, we could improve daily in Bible knowledge, prayer, devotional reading and other spiritual disciplines. Making a decision in the morning to *"kaizen"* in some area would not only help us to fight the natural tendencies toward laziness, but would eliminate wasted time and gain momentum as we pursue our goal of building our spiritual lives and loving God and people better.

If I were to tell you I will give you $86,400.00 every day from now on but under the condition that you have to spend the entire allotment of $86,400.00 each day in order to keep the money coming, do you think you could comply? God has given us 86,400 seconds every day – potential moments that pass through our lives that can either go unnoticed because they are so "little" or can, like Jonathan and his armor-bearer, end up being big divine moments that can change history. This is the secret to living the dream. As we abide in the joy of the Lord which is our strength (Neh. 8:10), and demonstrate His joy which is a fruit of the Spirit (Gal. 5:22), we will learn the secret of serving the Lord "with gladness" (Ps. 100:2). Some people serve the Lord with

> *Some people serve the Lord with gladness and some people just serve the Lord! The choice is ours.*

gladness and some people just serve the Lord! The choice is ours.

It seems logical that if God plans a wonderful life for us that the enemy of our souls (whom Jesus describes as a thief) would look for every opportunity to rob us of the wonder of this wonderful life. I would like to expose a few of those devices or schemes he uses to rob us of our joy.

The Devil's Dirty Tricks

Paul, portraying himself as a spiritual matchmaker, warned the Corinthian church about the craftiness of the serpent who had deceived Eve in the garden. Paul's desire to present them as a "pure virgin to Christ" was being threatened by a triple counterfeit: a false Jesus, a false spirit, and a false gospel. Knowing that the picture of a pure virgin brings to mind youth, hopefulness, innocence, simplicity, and joyful anticipation of marriage, he warned them about abandoning their "sincere and pure devotion to Christ" (2 Cor. 11:1-4). He was concerned that they would go after other lovers who would lead them away from Jesus.

The devil often comes with enticing words, but as "the father of lies," his intent is to kill, steal, and destroy (Jn. 10:10). Attacks usually come from three specific directions: attacks from outside (the world), attacks from inside (the flesh), and attacks from below (the devil). God's power is far greater than that of His enemy, and He has given us plenty of weapons to fend off any assaults. Our part is to be vigilant, always aware of the craftiness of the serpent – God's ever-present enemy.

Dirty Bombs

I once saw a television documentary in which the power of "dirty bombs" was illustrated by a computer image showing what would happen if a dirty bomb went off near the U.S. Capitol. The journalist explained that the dirty bomb's invisible and odorless cloud could kill anyone within its deadly reach. Even more terrifying was his warning that such a cloud could hang in the atmosphere for several days, paralyzing all in its wake.

I have met people who have had "dirty bombs" released in their spirits that rendered them ineffective for the kingdom of God and unable to live the dream. These detonate when mean, negative, critical, judgmental, and hurtful words penetrate our hearts. As we heed these negative words, our lives have the opposite effect than when we put our faith in God's Word. Psychologists estimate that it takes approximately six encouraging words to neutralize every discouraging, negative hit that we have taken in the form of a dirty bomb.

The Bible tells us to look into the mirror of God's Word and thus be changed from glory to glory into the image of Jesus Christ (2 Cor. 3:18). In other words, we need to ask God to dispel the cloud of spiritual radioactivity that is hanging onto our spirits because of the lies that have been spoken to us over the years. I have talked to young people whose fathers have told them they were a failure and they would never amount to anything. This rendered them nearly paralyzed in their spiritual and emotional formation.

There is no magic wand that someone can wave over your head to dispel the impact of dirty bombs. The only prescription is to start believing the truth and not let unbelief continue to spread the effects of the dirty bomb. "See to it brothers, that none of you has a sinful, unbelieving heart that turns away from the living God" (Heb. 3:12).

Dirty Birds

The great Protestant reformer Martin Luther once said, "You can't stop birds from flying over your head but you can keep them from building a nest in your hair!" He gave this as a word picture illustrating temptation. Temptation will come to all of us. Jesus Himself was tempted (Matt. 4, Lk. 4, Heb. 4:15), and all of us will enter into seasons of temptation – some worse than others. Temptations, according to Luther, are like little birds that fly over our heads. However, when we allow the temptations to take root in our hearts they produce the seeds of

The great Protestant reformer Martin Luther once said, "You can't stop birds from flying over your head but you can keep them from building a nest in your hair!"

death and build big "nests in our hair." When birds are used as an illustration in Scripture it is often referring to something hurtful or unclean (see Matt. 13:4, 19, Rev. 18:2).

The birds' nest illustration in Luther's theology emerged from a German concept called *anfechtungen.* Although the word is hard to translate across linguistic and cultural contexts, Luther's concept of *anfechtungen* was the series of temptations, trials, turmoil, various afflictions, and lack of peace that assailed him throughout his life. For Luther, the source of the *anfechtungen* was not that important. There were times when he knew his trials were from God, but felt like they were from Satan. He also spoke of *anfechtungen* coming from the world and his own nature.

Luther used extreme words to describe the pain of his soul, but always mentioned the deliverance from these extreme trials by the grace of God. Like Paul's thorn in the flesh, Luther saw his *anfechtungen* as an attack from Satan, but recognized it could be seen as a gift if he responded by applying God's Word to the temptation. He ultimately saw this as a description of the Christian life: a battle of the soul in which the Christian is required to live and respond by faith.

Song of Solomon 2 tells of "little foxes that ruin the vineyards," which is an apt metaphor for the way small temptations can destroy a thriving ministry. Shortly after the famous 1949 Los Angeles crusade in which Billy Graham was launched onto the national scene, he met with his team at a hotel in Modesto, CA. With wise foresight they prepared for the temptations that were likely to assail Billy as he was launched into worldwide prominence as an evangelist. As a result these four men entered into a covenant with each other called "The Modesto Manifesto" in which they made four simple commitments. They resolved to:

1. Not speak negatively or criticize others in public

2. To be accountable in finances and display integrity in their business standards

3. To tell the truth and report statistics honestly, allowing the churches to report the crusade results

4. To be exemplary in morals which included the agreement never to be alone in a room or car with a woman to avoid the appearance of impropriety

In this way the Graham team proactively kept the birds out of their hair for sixty years. In an era of religious scandal, Dr. Graham and his team have been a shining example of living lives above reproach and have truly finished strong.

Dirty Rats

Author C.S Lewis once wrote of a terrifying incident from his youth in North Ireland. While playing hide and seek, he ran to the basement entrance, flicked on the light and ran down the stairs, only to be confronted by a cadre of rats, who, likewise surprised to see him, scurried off into the darkness.

Lewis used this experience as an illustration of what some theologians have called "original sin" and "the fallen human nature." My purpose is not to quibble over how far we fell, when we fell, or how original our sin really is, but to point out that many of us have dark areas of our life that we are unaware of until something or someone "turns the light on."

I have counseled with many people who seem painfully unable to break a habitual sin in their life because they never called the divine exterminator when the rats first appeared. They not only allowed the rats to exist but actually fed the little buggers that were in their basement! Even when we do make the choice to repent of a given sin or habit, we can find it extremely difficult. To the degree that we "sow to the flesh," we will reap corruption and to the degree that we sow to the Spirit, we will reap life everlasting (Gal. 6:9, KJV).

Not long ago I was trying to help a young couple restore their marriage after the wife had been unfaithful. To her credit, she confessed her sin and attempted to rebuild the relationship. They went together for counseling and were moving forward when she hit the wall and "couldn't" reconcile. Feelings of emotional dependency on the other man were still nibbling at her heart. She needed to see that when rats in the basement are either tolerated or nourished they usually cannot be exterminated at once. To quote the prophet, "...they sow the wind, and they reap the whirlwind" (Hos. 8:7).

We all have dirty rats in our hearts. Lewis encouraged us to be humble about our shortcomings and acknowledge that even if the devil were to take a vacation, we still have to recognize along with the Apostle Paul that "…nothing good lives in me…" (Rom. 7:18). Periodically the Holy Spirit will allow a sudden flicking on of the light in our hearts, a sudden temptation to be angry, a look toward someone of the opposite sex that is inappropriate, an opportunity to fudge on taking money or time away from our employer, our church, or our ministry.

Rats are relatively small creatures and actually quite harmless if we keep our distance. But when we refuse to deal with the rats in the basement they can end up creating big problems for the whole household.

6

ROLE PRAYING

By now I hope you've seen that the key to the Next-Big-Thing lifestyle is simply obeying the next thing that God tells you to do. That is what makes it "big." As you do the will of God on a moment-by-moment basis, moments become hours, hours become days, weeks, and years, etc. The fruit of thousands of responses to opportunities to do the Next Big Thing is a truly divine legacy. I have told my wife that if I happen to "assume room temperature" before she does that I would like my epitaph to read, "A Friend of God and Sinners." This would encompass both my vertical and horizontal relationships and responsibilities on this planet.

The Christian life can be summarized by three simple words: Doing God's will. While many stress over this seemingly elusive, wonderful plan, I would like to suggest that the will of God is not that hard to find. This is simply because His will is rooted in His Character. God wants to guide you more than you want to be guided! Because He is a loving Father, He wants us to find His will more than we do, and it follows that He will make the finding of His will relatively easy. We just need to stay in touch. Hence, we need to develop and maintain our prayer life.

Like many people I have had great struggles becoming a man of prayer. As a Bible teacher and evangelist, I would go for days without any significant time of intercessory prayer or conversation with God. My quiet times were erratic, distracted, unfocused and, especially when embarked on early in the morning were interrupted by visits to sleepland. In fact my quiet times were extremely "quiet."

In the early 1980s I began to travel the world teaching seminars on personal evangelism and speaking at mission conferences. My anemic prayer life, however, gnawed at my conscience. It seemed easier to spend fifteen hours studying for my seminars than it was to spend fifteen minutes in prayer. So I attended a prayer seminar to alleviate this problem called "Could You Not Tarry One Hour?" The teacher suggested spending one hour in prayer a day using the Lord's Prayer as a paradigm. I faithfully applied the teaching – for about two weeks! Then I fell back into my prayer-less lifestyle.

Next I read Dick Eastman's book *No Easy Road* which, while admitting that a strong prayer life is no easy road, gave practical suggestions such as dividing the time into twelve five-minute slots consisting of worship, confession, intercession, thanksgiving, etc. This approach also lasted for a few weeks and than sputtered to a halt. I read books on prayer by Leonard Ravenhill, E.M. Bounds, and Joy Dawson. I even dove into the Catholic mystics like Teresa of Avila and Thomas A'Kempis. I tried prayer walking, but that wasn't very fruitful either, being distracted by birds, dogs, out-of-state license plates and bumper stickers! I don't have Attention Deficit Disorder – it's just that I pay attention to everything at once! So here I was a traveling preacher, leading a missionary training base, expected to be an authority on evangelism and missions – and my prayer life stunk! What's a struggling preacher to do?

Two things rescued me from my dilemma. First of all, the practice of spiritual journaling helped jump start my prayer life. Secondly, I developed a habit I have come to call "intentional thanksgiving."

The Joy of Journaling

My journey in journaling began when I discovered that YWAM had begun publishing an annual Prayer Diary. Its features included eight blank lines per day to record thoughts, prayers or items to pray for, a daily Bible reading schedule, and an unreached people group to pray for.

I bought my first prayer diary in 1983. I now own, as of this writing, 28 prayer diaries that sit on a shelf in my study, a continuous record of my spiritual progress or regress as the case may be. Just this morning I made an entry into my present prayer diary.

I began just writing down random thoughts as they came into my mind. Then I made long prayer lists because I was not praying as the Bible exhorts us to pray – specifically (Phil. 4:6-7). As I continued to make an intentional effort to implement *kaizen* into my prayer life, God continued to give me ways to bolster my time and enjoyment of His presence.

> *My prayer diaries are a continuous record of my spiritual progress or regress as the case may be.*

One day while grazing through the book of Proverbs, I slowed down on the well-known verse, "Trust in the Lord with all of your heart and lean not on your own understanding; in all your ways acknowledge him, and he will make your paths straight" (Prov. 3:5-6). Then I heard the Holy Spirit speak to my heart, "What are all your ways?" I began thinking about the various "roles" I play in life.

As I reflected on my spiritual, social and physical life, and the ministries God had led me in, they seemed to fall neatly into ten categories. To help remember them, I used a memory device called a mnemonic using the same letter to categorize each of the different roles I played. With me they all happen to begin with "P." I then broke them down into ten one-word headings which I began to insert regularly in my journal during daily prayer times. They are:

Piety[1] – I pray about my Christian character and do periodic "throne checks" (a self-examination to see if Jesus or self is on the throne of my life.)

Personal – I pray about my interaction with other people as well as personal disciplines like prayer, fasting, Bible study, memorization, meditation, diligence, planning, and time management.

Physical – I pray about areas having to do with my body – my health, my nutritional and exercise disciplines, as well as my sleep habits.

Progeny – I pray about my relationship with my wife, sons, and grandkids and as a son to my own father. I also fulfill my role of priestly intercession for those in my family.

Preaching – I ask God for diligence in study, wisdom, preparation, and power in preaching and any other ministry I have to people.

Personal Evangelism – I pray for spontaneous obedience to God's Spirit and love for and sensitivity to

---

[1] An old English word referring to spirituality

non-believers in my orbit. I also pray by name for those I've recently witnessed to.

Products – I pray for wisdom and revelation in my writing and other ministry materials that I make available, as well as finances for translation work, etc.

Position – This is my position of leadership in the body of Christ. I pray Solomon's prayer (1 Kings 3) for wisdom and the fear of the Lord because the lives of others are affected by my leadership.

Pioneering – I pray for anything I'm involved in regarding cross-cultural ministry and especially the starting of new ministries.

Provision – This is my "give us this day our daily bread" prayer. Having not received a salary for the last thirty years has kept me on my knees for both ministry and family needs.

You may not have ten "P's" for your "ways." You may have five or six or you may have fifteen or sixteen. I simply want to encourage you to spend some time alone with the Lord, waiting on Him. I have implemented this device in my life in an attempt to *acknowledge God in all my ways* (Prov. 3:6) and glorify Him in everything I do (1 Cor. 10:31). During my devotional time I try to be sensitive to His Spirit and wait on Him as I pray through these different areas. One day the Lord may be emphasizing the Piety area and dealing with me in areas of pride or anger that may have manifested the previous day or two. On another day He may speak to me in the area of Progeny (family) and tell me to send a gift to my grandkids. In the Physical area, He may remind me to avoid junk food or get more exercise.

Once while on a fasting and prayer time in Fiji, I came to the Provision section and sensed the Lord speaking to me to pray for finances to purchase a house. Not only did I not have any money to buy a house, but I live in a state (Hawaii) which has some of the highest real estate prices in the country. Nevertheless in obedience to the Holy Spirit I prayed that God would provide a home for my family. Within a week I received a phone call from a businessman I knew from a church where I speak occasionally. He got right to the point: "Danny, are you praying to be able to buy a house?" I quickly responded, "If you had asked me that question two weeks ago I would have said, 'No.'" I then told him about the word that came to me while I was in Fiji. "Good," he said, "This confirms what I felt the Lord leading me to do. You'll be receiving a check in the mail for $31,000 to get you started on a down payment for the house. I sold one of my businesses and was impressed by the Lord to send you a tithe from the sale."

Wow, did that build our faith! Linda and I gave away $3,100 as a tithe and put the rest in the bank. One miracle followed another and within a few months, we purchased a beautiful home. Would I still be sitting in this house today if I hadn't divided my life up into these various roles and prayed into them? Perhaps, but I don't think so. The Bible indicates we should pray specifically. This type of discipline helps me to keep up-to-date on prayer needs because it forces me to write things down and focus on acknowledging God in all my "ways."

Journaling helps us to record in detail God's dealings with us and leaves us with valuable instructions for the future. Once, I was severely betrayed by someone. "Stabbed in the back" would be an appropriate word picture. My journal records my not-too spiritual but honest responses to this hurt. The following are some journal entries during those weeks of "recovery." First, there was anger ("Lord I feel like punching him in the mouth!"), then confession ("I hate him for doing this to me"), then petition ("Hatred is a sin. Help me to forgive…"). A few days into this trial my journal records: "I spent ninety minutes

> *My journal looked me in the eye every morning and forced me to confront myself and eventually, I got the victory.*

today on my knees with Matthew 5:44 – '...love your enemies...' He is not my enemy, Lord. He is my brother. Would You help me to love him."

It took about two weeks of daily seeking the Lord, being honest with my feelings and writing them down, for me to forgive this fellow from my heart. My journal looked me in the eye every morning and forced me to confront myself and eventually, I got the victory.

Intentional Thanksgiving

In addition to journaling, my prayer life has benefitted greatly from an understanding I received while reading in the Psalms one day. In a short Psalm, a little phrase seemed to leap off the page and into my spirit: "Enter his gates with thanksgiving and his courts with praise..." (Ps. 100:4). Key word: *Enter*. I began to experiment with a time of intentional thanksgiving, writing down various things in my life that I was grateful for.

If my mind wandered or I was tempted to approach God like some sort of divine Santa Claus, I would discipline my soul to slow down and get grateful. If I ran out of things to be grateful for, I would start at the top of my head and work down: "Thank You Lord for my hair, my brain, for eyes to see, and ears to hear. Thank You for my heart, lungs, arms, legs, toes… By this time I'm on a roll, and I thank and praise Him for my salvation, family, home, car, food, and for all His divine interventions in my life.

All this thanksgiving causes my heart to burst forth in praise to the One who has done so much for me through His grace. I am now entering His courts with praise. The gates are the entry point and the courts are the privileged positions of the servants of the king. Another help in my prayer life is a song book I picked up at a garage sale (one of the best investments I ever made). It contains over 600 biblically based hymns and choruses that assist me in entering and staying in His courts.

George Mueller, whose trust in God for the care of hundreds of British orphans is legendary, wrote in his autobiography, "…I saw more clearly than ever, that the first great primary business which I ought to attend every day was, to have my soul happy in the Lord.

"…I saw more clearly than ever, that the first great primary business which I ought to attend every day was, to have my soul happy in the Lord."

The first thing to be concerned about was not how I might serve the Lord, but how I might get my soul into a happy state and how my inner man might be nourished…"

Following Mueller's lead, shortly after my feet hit the floor in the morning, I direct my initial prayers to God Himself and what He has done for me. I not only get a jump start on the day, but also get my soul into a "happy state." Through much trial and a lot of error I have greatly improved my prayer life. I'm still not where I want to be, but I am a long way from where I was. I am beginning to declare with David, more from delight than duty that, "One thing I asked of the Lord, this is what I seek; that I may dwell in the house of the Lord all the days of my life, to gaze upon the beauty of the Lord and to seek Him in His temple" (Ps. 27:4).

Fast and Focus Day

Each year in early January, I pack up my Bible, prayer diaries from the previous and new year, and a large bottle of water. I go to a secluded place for a day of prayer and fasting. When I arrive, I force myself to settle down and be still before God (Ps. 46:10). I like to think of my soul much like a fishbowl all stirred up by activity that needs time to just chill and settle down. I then slowly read my journal entries from the previous year and evaluate my life. Socrates once said, "The unexamined life is not worth living," and I have taken that to heart. There is always the temptation to become neurotic in self-criticism. However, I find that a yearly time of healthy introspection is good for the soul (see 2 Cor. 13:5).

During my initial time of reflection, I look for habit patterns that I have developed, good or bad, and make adjustments. For instance, if I have gained weight, I may set a goal in the coming year to lose it. If I had set a goal the previous year to read the Bible through and failed due to a lack of self-discipline, I adjust to meet that goal in the coming year. Setting attainable, intentional and measurable goals in all ten roles I play in life I keep myself busy all day, as I fast, pray, and focus on my progress as a child of God. It is simply a way of keeping the instrument God has given me – body, soul, and spirit – finely tuned. Charles Spurgeon pointed out that Michelangelo was diligent to make his own brushes in order that he could perfect his artistic craft.[2] We would do well to follow his lead.

One of my mentors is Joy Dawson, an eighty-four-year-old radical prayer warrior for God. She was once asked by an inquiring young leader how she had the time to pray over her life in such detail. She responded with a combination of grandmotherly kindness and prophetic punch by saying, "My dear, I seek God in detail because I

---

[2]Charles H. Spurgeon, *Lectures to My Students* (Grand Rapids: Zondervan, 1954), 7

don't have the time for the confusion and wasted time that is the result of not seeking Him in detail." Such attention to detail may seem overwhelming or even legalistic, but it helps me obey Peter's instruction to "…make your calling and election sure" (2 Pet. 1:10).

The Bible tells us that we are God's *poema* or "work of art" (Eph. 2:10), and it follows that it is our responsibility to provide Him with our tools in the best possible condition. This type of "discipline for the purpose of godliness" (1 Tim. 4:7, NASB) is sure to prepare us for the Next Big Thing.

The Bible tells us that we are God's poema or "work of art" (Eph. 2:10), and it follows that it is our responsibility to provide Him with our tools in the best possible condition.

One of the goals of the yearly Fast and Focus Day is being confident of being in the will of God and ready for the Next Big Thing. By knowing God's will, many guidance decisions can be made quickly. For instance, a few years ago a local tourist ministry called me and asked me to consider becoming their new director. I immediately said no. They were surprised that I didn't even say I would pray about it.

They told me they had gotten my name in prayer and thought perhaps I was the man for the job. I simply said, "I don't need to pray about this request because I KNOW that God hasn't called me to a tourist ministry. This is because I have spent much time seeking God on what He is calling me to do, and I know that doesn't fit. May the Lord bless you as you find a new director."

The Germans have a word, *sitz im leben*, which refers to our "setting, [or place] in life." Once we know our *sitz im leben*, we are free from the tyranny of constantly wondering about God's will for our lives. We find rest by being content with where God has placed us.

As we spend time thanking God, praying over our roles, and inviting the Holy Spirit to guide and empower us, we thus "acknowledge him in all of our ways" (Prov. 3:6) and find great security in that place. "As a bird wanders from its nest, so is a man who wanders from his place" (Prov. 27:8 KJV).

7

MAKING HISTORY

"The past is history, the future's a mystery. It's what's happening now that is important. That's why they call it the 'present.'" This famous quote of unknown origin begs the question: Can what we do in the present affect the future? Can we change history?

One of my favorite worship songs has as its chorus:

"I'm gonna be a history maker in this land.
I'm gonna be a speaker of truth to all mankind…"

Are these words, penned by Delirious band member Martin Smith, accurate? Is it possible for us to change the world? If we look back to the Butterfly Effect, you are changing the world every day whether you know it or not. The people within the circle of your Next-Big-Thing lifestyle are continually influenced either for good or for bad. So you are making history. That's why it's so important what you do with your life right NOW.

A few years ago, Naomi Peachey was eight years old and living north of London when she felt that God was speaking to her about taking care of orphans. She shared her impressions with her parents, John and Suzi, and little sister, Lily.

The family asked God what they could do to help orphans, then proceeded to pray and to work, one little step at a time. John and Suzi did research while the girls sold greeting cards, salad dressing, and toys to make money for the poor. Meanwhile, God was downloading into their hearts and minds more ideas on how to set up a ministry for orphans.

They recruited other helpers – social workers, book-keepers and those who could help with micro-enterprise options and income generation loans to those who would adopt the orphans. They were guided by Psalm 68:5-6 which says, the Lord is "a father to the fatherless, a defender of widows…God sets the lonely in families…" Their goal was that the children would feel they belonged to a family rather than part of an institution.

They were directed to Sam and Irene Kisolo, Ugandans who had taken into their home sixteen children whose parents died of AIDS. In the Ugandan village of Jinja, the Peacheys launched Orphans Know More (OKM), coordinating the effort with many other volunteers. They produced a video documenting the plight of some twelve million

African AIDS orphans. At this writing, 138 children have been given "a face, a family, and a future" along with financial assistance. OKM continues to grow and spread awareness of what has become a worldwide problem. It all began with a little girl's prayer, but as the late Dr. Francis Schaeffer wrote, "There are no little people and no little places."

When I directed the Honolulu YWAM base in the late 1980s, a young woman named Andrea joined our staff. She often sat at our outdoor picnic tables next to a couple of telephone booths that were on our property. She did not eavesdrop, but one day she overheard the cries of fifteen-year-old Kelly, who lived next door to our ministry base.

She tenderly asked what was wrong, and Kelly shared how she had gotten pregnant and was considering an abortion. Andrea spent several days talking and praying with her. She eventually talked Kelly out of getting the abortion. A little girl was born, who now is in her 20s and along with her mom attends a church in Honolulu. Andrea did the Next Big Thing – that was to respond to someone in need and a life was literally saved. Now everyone who is affected for the good by Kelly's daughter continues the Butterfly Effect for God. Andrea changed history.

Another more famous history maker was a school teacher named Joshua Chamberlain who enlisted in the Union Army during the U.S. Civil War. On the second day of the Battle of Gettysburg, Colonel Chamberlain, commander of the 20th Maine, was ordered to hold the Confederate armies off of their extreme left flank at all cost. Chamberlain's superior, Colonel Strong Vincent, was killed shortly after he gave that command, but Chamberlain was determined to obey it and dug in on the ridge of "Little Round Top."

Soldiers of the 15th and 47th Alabama attacked five times in their attempt to overcome the left flank and gain a strategic advantage on the other union forces down the line. On the fourth charge, Chamberlain took a bullet – to his belt buckle. He fell down but got back up and kept fighting. The rebels retreated.

After the fifth charge, with ammunition running low and darkness closing in, Chamberlain knew his eighty men couldn't withstand another attack by the 400 Rebel soldiers below. In that moment, he made a decision. He called down the line for his men to fix bayonets. Then he jumped over the wall and yelled, "Charge!" before his lieutenants could stop his apparent insanity and talk him out of such a reckless move! His eighty men ran down the hill and took the Confederate Army by surprise, capturing almost all of the 400 soldiers in the valley below.

Many historians believe that if Chamberlain had not charged that day, the South would have won the Battle of

Gettysburg. And if the South had won at Gettysburg, they would have likely won the war. If they had won the war, there would be no United States of America today, as we know it. Consequently there would have been no nation strong enough to withstand Hitler, the Russians, etc. The big picture of history has been painted, but it started with a decision by a school teacher in the evening hours of July 2, 1863. (During the writing of this book I was privileged to visit the Gettysburg battlefield and stand on the very spot where Colonel Vincent fell and Chamberlain gave his command).

The average person makes 1,800 decisions a day. Some are inconsequential, like which pen I decided to use to edit this manuscript. Others, particularly ones that involve clear obedience to God, are much more crucial. David declared these choices were worthy of "great reward" (Ps. 19:11).

My personal history was affected by a quick decision made by a German commanding officer in 1944. Sargent Carl Lehmann, was pinned down in a firefight outside Rome and forced to surrender along with twenty of his U.S. Army Ranger comrades. Before his capture, he buried his knife, wrist watch and a captured German luger, but forgot to empty his pockets of "scalps" – winged-shaped souvenirs that he had taken from dead Nazi soldiers he'd found in a bunker. When a trigger-happy German guard discovered the scalps, he moved Carl away from the other prisoners.

The guard, who "looked to be about fifteen," begged the *Feldwebel* (officer-in-charge) for permission to shoot Carl, but he was denied it. Carl later said, "I was blessing the *Feldwebel's* obviously sainted mother for having birthed him. Before we were marched out, the Feldwebel came close and smiled at me. 'You haff a Churman name, Carl.' That and what went before was worth the snappy salute I delivered and which he returned."[1]

We don't know if the *Feldwebel* survived the war. If he did, he probably wouldn't even remember the incident of the over-zealous Nazi kid with the pistol. It was a little decision for him, but a mighty big one for Carl and his son born several years later. By the way, Carl was captured three times by his enemies and escaped thrice as well – the last of which was for good, and so I am here to tell the story!

> When we are able by God's grace to find ourselves in the center of His will, filled with His Spirit, and responding to the next thing He tells us to do, it's then we make history.

[1]H. Paul Jeffers, *Onward We Charge. The Historic Story of Darby's Rangers in World War II* (New York: NAL Caliber, 2007), 235-243

It's these big/little decisions I am focusing on. When we are able by God's grace to find ourselves in the center of His will, filled with His Spirit, and responding to the next thing He tells us to do, it's then we make history. Paul told the Colossians to make the most of every opportunity (Col. 4:5). When we do, we can be a catalyst for altering the future.

Stuck in a Moment

"Therefore since we are surrounded by such a great cloud of witnesses, let us throw off everything that hinders and the sin that so easily entangles, and let us run with perseverance the race marked out for us. Let us fix our eyes on Jesus the author and perfecter of our faith who for the joy set before him endured the Cross, scorning its shame and sat down at the right hand of the throne of God" (Heb. 12:1, 2). The writer to the Hebrews had just listed in Chapter 11 the exploits of a large number of Next-Big-Thing heroes. Chapter twelve begins by likening God's plan for us to a marathon race. The key to success in this race is "fixing our eyes on Jesus," who reminds us of both the hindrances and assistances to finishing our race with joy.

A couple of thousand years before Nike and Adidas designed ultra-lightweight running shorts, athletes would have to "throw off" everything that hindered them from running their fastest race. This would include the long, cumbersome togas that folks wore in those days. Following are some "weights" that can slow us down in our pursuit of the finish line.

The writer of Hebrews makes it obvious that sin can entangle and hinder us in our running. However, he distinguishes sin from other "things" that handicap our ability to race effectively. I call these freeze points.[2] They are strongholds formed in the mind which immobilize and hinder us from running God's race. While these strongholds may be fortified and fed by satanic influences, God puts the responsibility on the Christian to "...demolish arguments and every pretension that sets itself up against the knowledge of God, and we take captive every thought to make it obedient to Christ" (2 Cor. 10:5).

Freeze Points

Bono and the Edge, of the rock group U2, penned a song which describes a girl who is "stuck in a moment" and loses her ability to function:

> "You've got stuck in a moment and now you can't get
> out of it

---

[2] A term borrowed from John Trent's book, *Lifemapping.*

Don't say that later will be better
Now you're stuck in a moment
And you can't get out of it."

"And if the night runs over and if the day won't last
And if your way should falter along the stony pass
It's just a moment, this time will pass."

So how do these strongholds or freeze points form? Often they are negative messages that register in our minds because of past hurts. In my work with Youth With A Mission, I have counseled young women who through clenched teeth have said things like, "I will never trust another man." When I ask why, they typically tell me about an absent and uncaring father, abusive uncle, hypocritical youth pastor, or deceptive boyfriend. I can understand why a girl would make such a statement, but until she can grant forgiveness that stronghold will freeze her at the starting line and rob her of the joy of both running and finishing the race.

The positive and negative experiences of our relationships are recorded in our hearts and minds like stories written on paper. When someone has hurt us, we clutch onto that paper to try to find hope there. But when we build up bitterness, resentment or hatred it is like someone sets fire to our piece of paper as we continue to hold onto it. Our hand burns and we cry out in pain, all the while refusing to let go of the paper! Until we release the person with forgiveness, the hurt will go on and it will freeze us at the starting line of God's race for us.

Flash Points

Another factor to succeed in the race is perseverance. I have run many cross-country, track, and marathon races in my life. Since I lack "fast-twitch" muscles (needed for sprinting), long-distance races have always been my forte. The key to winning long-distance races is endurance and that takes time and training. Perseverance is the non-negotiable ingredient to finishing our life's race with joy. While freeze points hinder us from running the race, flash points are those events in our lives that feed our faith. They help us to look back on God's faithfulness in the past to have the faith to finish well in the future.

> *Perseverance is the non-negotiable ingredient to finishing our life's race with joy. While freeze points hinder us from running the race, flash points are those events in our lives that feed our faith.*

This is illustrated in the Old Testament by the "stones of remembrance." God told Joshua to instruct his leaders to erect a monument to God's faithfulness to help them cross the Jordan River (Josh. 4). The same principle is given to us by what Samuel called the "Ebenezer stone" (1 Sam. 7:12). Reflecting on God's faithfulness to us in the past ignites a spark (or a "flash") in our hearts that fuels the perseverance we need to finish the race. When I look back on my life I remember these flash points: an encouraging sentence, a statement by a spiritual leader, a word directly from the Lord, or a time when God blew my mind with His faithfulness that I needed to intentionally <u>remember.</u> Entering them in my journal has helped keep these personal history-making events accessible to me when I need a "second wind" in the race of life. These are my Ebenezer stones – stones of remembrance.

About two weeks after I gave my life to Jesus, I was sitting on the 26th Ave. Beach in Santa Cruz, CA reading my pocket New Testament. I was still suffering from LSD flashbacks, a serious loss of memory and a self-image that was circling the drain! It was almost in a "flash" that a verse in Ephesians about God cleansing the church with "the washing of water by the Word" (Eph.5:26) seemed to spring up off the page. I believe God spoke to me through that verse that He was going to heal my mind through a constant diet of His Word. It was then that I began reading, memorizing, and meditating on the Bible for hours every day and saw the Lord heal my brain. That's a stone of remembrance.

A few years later in a conversation with a spiritual leader named Kalafi Moala, he said, "Danny, you have a burden for souls – that's good. But God wants you to think nations." Those few words ignited a spark in my spirit and the last nearly thirty years of my life have been committed to world missions. It took less than ten seconds to utter those life-changing words. It was a flash point.

I encourage you to chronicle instances like these when God speaks a clear word to you or shows Himself faithful. The memory of these flash points will help you overcome past hurts, wounds, lies, and obstacles in our walk with the Lord. This simple discipline builds perseverance.

Field Points

Once freeze points have begun to thaw and flash points have ignited faith, we need to simply discover the general pattern of God's will for us and then the specific design that He has for us. Several helps are available to us from different sources. There is the "Original Design" course, Saddleback Church's "SHAPE" seminar, and various types of spiritual and motivational gift discovery tests, etc. I am not so concerned on how you discover God's design for you - just that you do it! In Peter's final letter to us, he told us to make our calling and election sure (2 Peter 1:10). What is the field that God has called you to labor in? What is the sphere of society that He has called you to influence? Who are the people that He has primarily called you to be a bless-

> *What is the field that God has called you to labor in? What is the sphere of society that He has called you to influence?*

ing to? Which nation does He want you to contribute to its discipling?

In addition to the above self-discovery courses, I have found a helpful paradigm for finding God's will that I call "Five Finger Guidance." When faced with decisions regarding direction for myself and family, I hold up my hand and run through five scriptural checkpoints:

First, of course, I look to the Bible. Often through daily Bible reading we develop a frame of reference that helps us judge other leadings or impulses we may feel. Many guidance decisions are simply applying the Bible's wisdom and going for it. Secondly, we must attune our spiritual senses to discern God's voice. This guidance may, at times, be confirmed by checkpoint number three – circumstances. These, however, are not an absolute litmus test for God's leading, because at times He may speak to us to do seemingly foolish things, like march around a city (Joshua 6) or dip in a river seven times (2 Kings 5)!

The final two checkpoints are seeking godly counsel and supernatural guidance in the form of visions, dreams and, "words of knowledge" (see 1 Corin. 12:8, KJV).

Mike Casey, a former hard-drinking, hard-partying sailor, was a student in the Discipleship Training School in Honolulu. One day in 1994 while he was eating lunch alone seated at an outdoor picnic table, a man suddenly approached and told him God wanted Mike to start an orphanage in the Philippines. Mike's read on this was that it was an angel, a messenger from God who was concerned for the orphans in the Philippines. Today, Mike and his Filipina bride Nollie oversee three orphanages and have seen scores of girls' lives transformed. The Five Finger Guidance is then confirmed by God's peace that serves as a "referee" in our hearts (see Col. 3:15).

The Christian life is a marathon, not a sprint. As a marathon runner myself, I freely acknowledge there's pain in the race, but there's also joy. When we pursue the Next-Big-Thing lifestyle we can have confident expectation that there is "joy set before us," at the end of the race (Heb. 12:2). The Bible tells us the "joy of the Lord is our strength" (Neh. 8:10); in His presence "is fullness of joy;" at His right hand are "pleasures forevermore" (Ps. 16:11,

KJV); and that joy is one of the main fruits of the Spirit that God seeks to grow within our lives (Gal. 5:22).

There is no greater sense of joy and peace than to know that we are smack dab in the center of God's will, with the people that He wants us to be with, at

There is no greater sense of joy and peace than to know that we are smack dab in the center of God's will...

the right time and place, doing the right thing and watching God move on our behalf in this "field."

I must caution, however, that many well-meaning men and women have lost their joy and suffered from the inevitable burn out, blow up or break down that accompanies doing God's will outside of God's ways. His way is the way of grace, the way of the easy yoke (Matt. 11:18-30). Are you consistently overwhelmed, exhausted, and frustrated at doing much, but accomplishing little? Do you feel like you are always pushing up hill? You may need to take a time out and ask God if you have gotten off track somehow. If your yoke is hard, it's most likely not Jesus' yoke. As my YWAM friend Dean Sherman has said, "Jesus never burned anybody out!"

My wife Linda and I thank God on a regular basis for the "fit" that we have found in the field that He has called us to. In the beginning of my spiritual journey, I was a bit insecure about what exactly God was calling me to do. During my initial rehab, I worked with my hands and found one of my first ministry responsibilities was the pick up, delivery, and daily cleaning of over forty portable toilets so that 3,000 people at a Jesus Festival could have somewhere to relieve themselves (this was after I humbly volunteered to preach a plenary session, although I was just a few months old in my faith). While assisting the "Honey Bucket Man" in vacuuming out these portable toilets in over 100 degree heat in a barren field in Northern California, God spoke to me and said, "Welcome to the ministry!" It was then that I saw that serving in the most menial of tasks and being faithful to do the Next Big Thing was the essence of ministry. I concluded that God was calling me to be a deacon (one who serves in practical ways), and I was okay with that.

Along with God's revelation to me about faithfulness in my Next Big Thing (as in cleaning toilets), He showed more specific arenas of faithfulness that He wanted me to explore. Shortly after my conversion, I started witnessing on the streets and to this day, I still go witnessing on a regular basis. However, I am not primarily a street evangelist. Street preaching just wasn't my main "fit."

I also began teaching high school Bible studies, but found that I didn't quite fit the profile of the typical youth pastor. Many of my friends were starting churches with the young converts from the Jesus Movement, but I soon discovered I was neither a church planter nor a pastor.

During my Fast and Focus days I would seek the Lord to find my one "call." When I was first recruited into YWAM, I presumed God wanted me to be a missionary. My wife and I had our sights set on working among Hindus in Fiji. We spent seven months in Fiji but still, no "fit." I finally got the understanding that God wanted me to be a multifaceted minister of the Gospel – not exclusively a pastor, missionary, Bible teacher, youth pastor, deacon or street evangelist, but that He had indeed called me to all these things. Then he led me to start writing books! When I complained about feeling like a "jack of all trades and master of none," God assured me with a word which became the key point of this book – that is, "Do the Next Big Thing I put in front of you!"

One day, several years ago I was grazing through the book of Nehemiah and found my eyes lighting on a verse that said, *"Baruch, the son of Zabbai zealously repaired another section [of the wall]…"* (Neh. 3:20). In my mind's eye I saw a picture of a zealous little Jewish man diligently doing his thing. He was doing a little thing that contributed to a great task – the rebuilding of the walls of Jerusalem under Nehemiah's leadership. All of us have part of the wall to repair, a part of God's kingdom to labor in, and a part of God's family to belong to. Happy is the person that finds himself doing the Next Big Thing in God's appointed field.

8

SWEAT THE SMALL STUFF

I have a colleague in ministry who I have grown to love and respect as one of the foremost missionary statesmen on the planet today. He runs a BIG (there's that word again!) ministry that includes, among many other things, the recruitment and support of nearly 20,000 native church planters working throughout Asia.

I first met K.P. Yohannan in 1981, shortly after he had relocated to Texas to begin Gospel for Asia. I was impressed by K.P.'s simplicity and his passion for reaching, not only his native India but all Asia for Christ. Several years went by before I met K.P. again, this time at a missionary conference in Haryana, India, where both of us were speaking.

In the meantime K.P. had written a best-selling book called *Revolution in World Missions* which promoted the training, supporting, and sending of "native workers" to do missionary work. One evening, as we sat in the back of a car on our way back to our accommodations, I tried to engage him in a discussion on what I perceived to be his overemphasis on native missionaries that I saw to be at the expense of Western missionary support. I braced myself for an argument, but K.P. responded with a Christ-like humility and brokenness over what he had said and written in the past. He assured me that he believes that all of us, whether native or not, need to work together for the cause of Christ worldwide. He said there is room for everyone: long-term, short-term, red and yellow, black and white in God's missionary task.

The reason I bring up my relationship with K.P. in a book on the Next Big Thing is that the ministry of Gospel for Asia is a classic example of the main point of this book. The best "big things" are simply a combination of many small things that contribute to the bigness and quality of any endeavor.

Without exception, any time I have encountered the staff or volunteers from Gospel for Asia, I have observed an almost identical spirit of humility and servanthood in its people. In them I consistently experienced the love and kindness of God and other practical expressions of the fruit of God's Spirit. Often when I'm speaking to them on the phone and find myself in a bit of a hurry (after all I have to be busy evangelizing the world!), they tend to be peaceful, un-frantic, and always eager to pray for me and my needs.

I have never asked the Gospel for Asia leaders whether this attitude or spirit in their ministry is caught or taught. My guess would be it is mostly caught. A look at their daily schedule, whether at their missionary training centers in India or the American hub in Texas, reveals a strong emphasis on prayer, humility, serving, and submission to one another. My friends at Gospel for Asia – even though they would blush to hear me say it – are some of my foremost heroes in the body of Christ. They are unsung and unknown heroes and would probably like to keep it that way, but I have chosen to blow their cover because they model Jesus so well and the Next-Big-Thing lifestyle!

One of the best-selling devotional books of all time is *Practicing the Presence of God* by Brother Lawrence, a seventeenth century Carmelite Monk. His bottom line on abiding in God's presence was not today's incessant, almost neurotic, chasing after religious heebie-jeebies so that we "feel" Him. Lawrence was labeled by many as a mystic, however, he saw (and no doubt felt) God in the very mundane, rhythmic, normal routines of life. Here are just a few gems from his treasure trove of practical wisdom:

> *Lawrence…saw (and no doubt felt) God in the very mundane, rhythmic, normal routines of life.*

"We ought not to be weary doing little things for the love of God, who regards not the greatness of the work, but the love with which it is performed...It is not needful to have great things to do...we can do little things for God; I turn the cake that is frying for the love of Him, and that done, if there is nothing else to call me I prostrate myself in worship before Him, who has given me grace to work; afterward I rise happier than a King. It is enough for me to pick up but a straw from the ground for the love of God."[1]

So I would suggest that we have a need to indeed "sweat the small stuff" and to concentrate on the little things in our Christian life. We need to focus on what Pastor John Vawter writes about in his book, *Uncommon Graces* – kindness, mercy, loyalty, honesty, etc. Christian maturity has been described as "mastering the basics" and these are the basics.

> *...we have a need to indeed "sweat the small stuff" and to concentrate on the little things in our Christian life.*

Another thought-provoking book, *Flickering Pixels*, by a young Mennonite pastor named Shane Hipps, describes

---

[1] Brother Lawrence, *The Practice of the Presence of God with Spiritual Maxims* (Grand Rapids: Spire Books, 1967)

how our culture has become entranced by pixilated light. More and more of our time is spent gazing into the light of our television, computer monitor, iphone, and video game screens. The obvious selling point of these technologies is that we can get more accomplished in a shorter period of time. Hence we can get bigger faster.

As cool as these tools are, I believe we need to slow this train down and count the cost of what this uncontrolled pursuit of technology is costing us in basic relational skills. For example, a young woman named Sarah told her friend Kim she was going in for a biopsy and expressed her fear of having cancer. However, Sarah never followed up to tell Kim the results of the biopsy. When a month had gone by, Kim finally called her. Sarah replied glibly: "I'm so surprised you didn't know. I posted it on Facebook two weeks ago. The results were negative so I've been rejoicing ever since!" Kim was offended because Sarah had reached out to her so personally and privately when she was hurting, but shared her good news publicly, expecting that Kim would read her Facebook entry.

Even as we grow in our understanding of technology we must not let the flickering pixels take over our lives at the expense of some of the basics of the Christian life that will never change, no matter how technologically advanced we become. People need people.

First-Love Living

The book of Ephesians has been called "The Queen of the Epistles," "the crown of Saint Paul's writings," and "the most mature of all of Paul's works." Church father John Calvin called it his favorite letter. Ephesians is a treasure house of spiritual truth. The first three chapters detail at least forty-two separate spiritual blessings that we have by the grace of God in Christ. Chapters four through six contain some of the most practical, down-to-earth, nuts-and-bolts instructions on how to live the Christian life. The book ends with Paul's wisdom on how to wage warfare against the powers of darkness.

When Paul first visited Ephesus, amazing miracles took place there. Less than thirty years after Paul's writing of Ephesians, the church there was disintegrating. Jesus had identified in them a cancer that if not excised would cause Him to remove His presence from their midst (Rev. 2:1-7). What was this fatal disease? Idolatry, sexual immorality, racism, or some other macro-sin? No. Jesus simply said to them, *"You have*

> *... they had stopped sweating the small stuff, the simple stuff, the basics. Somehow in their pursuit of truth they had forgotten how to love.*

forsaken your first love." In other words, they had stopped sweating the small stuff, the simple stuff, the basics. Somehow in their pursuit of truth they had forgotten how to love.

Once I was confronted with accusations of heresy, lying, and blasphemy by a self-proclaimed watchdog over God's flock. Because I wouldn't "repent," he proceeded to spread his dirt on me publicly. I met with him privately to correct him. He continued to hurl his unpleasant vibes at me, to which I responded with the second step described in Matthew 18:16 to take him before two or three witnesses – in this case two pastors. He refused to back down. Realizing that I couldn't persuade him with argument, I simply said, "Bro, where's the love?!"

Without blinking an eye he turned to me, pointed his bony prophet-like finger in my face and said, "I don't care about love. I care about truth!" All the two pastors and I could do at this point was roll our eyes and say, "Bless his heart" (a nice Christian way of saying, "You just don't get it"). My well-meaning accuser failed to recognize that we must speak the truth in love (Eph. 4:15). My attempt to get him to submit his personal understanding of truth to the testimony of at least two or three witnesses infuriated him even more. The Bible declares that our anger does not bring about God's justice (Jas. 1:20), and that love is the greatest virtue (1 Cor. 13:13). My accuser thought he had truth, but lacked the greatest virtue, love. He, like the Ephesians, had become good at hating and bad at loving. My challenge was to love him anyway – not an easy task. As Jesus reminds us, it's easy to love those who love us but what about our enemies? Loving our enemies is included in our returning to first-love living.

> *He, like the Ephesians, had become good at hating and bad at loving.*

With Jesus' strong emphasis on loving God and loving our neighbors, that should be what the church is known for. Instead, the world is exposed to our lack of love through our thousands of church splits, doctrinal infighting, accusations over the airwaves and Internet, as well as our jealousies, gossip and other unloving activities. All these testify that we have forgotten to master the basics. Without love, everything is nothing.

So often, earnest followers of Christ dissect Bible books and verses much like a high school biology student would dissect a frog. They then come up with a certain "systematic" theology usually named after their favorite systematizer (think Calvin, Arminius, Wesley, Scofield, Ryrie, MacArthur, Sproul/Reformation, etc). Yet we all read the same Bible which warns against following after BIG names (1 Cor.

3:1-10). This is not to say that it's wrong to have favorite teachers. The danger comes when we buy into a certain "system" and when others disagree with us or have a different system, we take off the gloves and get ready to fight. According to Paul, if our system doesn't point us to love God and neighbor it is worth exactly nothing (1 Cor. 13). Thankfully, God gave the backsliding church at Ephesus four principles on how to return to first-love living.

Remember

"Remember the height from which you have fallen!"
(Revelation 2:5).

Genesis 1:26 says we were created in God's likeness. Along with our *imago dei* (image of God) comes the divine gift of memory. He gave this amazing gift not just to help us remember birthdays, pass tests in school or find our way home, but as an important tool of spiritual growth. Throughout the Bible God gives us clear reminders to remember His faithfulness. He gave Israel feasts like Pentecost, Passover, Tabernacles, and Purim so the Jews might *remember* these interventions of God on their behalf. Throughout the Books of Moses there are exhortations to remember not only their bondage in Egypt, but God's faithfulness to their nation during its forty years wandering in the wilderness (Deut. 8:2, 15:15). (I heard one Bible teacher suggest that one of the side benefits of God choosing to give Abraham the covenant of circumcision was so that every time he relieved himself he would be reminded of God's faithfulness – several times a day!) Jesus' key phrase in his farewell address to the disciples was to take the Eucharist *"in remembrance of Me"* (Lk. 22:19). I thank God for restoring my short-term memory – damaged by abuse of psychedelic drugs during my teenage years – for I want to always remember His faithfulness.

Speaking of memory, I invite you to meditate on this song written by a friend some years ago. Like God speaking to the Ephesians, it calls us back to our first love:

Crosses In The Sand

(Rob Mehl, 1973, Choral Seas Music)

"Wish I was a kid again, had the faith of a little child
When love and joy and honesty were part of my lifestyle,
When trees were green, the sky was blue, and I was in love
with everything,
All day long I'd think about the songs we used to sing.

Oh those were the days I loved my Savior so
My faith was plain and simple, and it was fun to watch
it grow,

I'd walk along the seashore drawing crosses in the sand
Dream of loving Jesus and holding His hand.

If I was a kid again I might do things differently
As far as holding on to love goes and growing up peacefully,
'Cause somewhere in the last few years
It seems like things have changed,
And my sense of priorities somehow I rearranged.

I'll never be a kid again, but the faith of a little child
Can well up deep inside of me and take over my lifestyle.
I'll get back to my first love, and love the One who loved
* me first;*
Let Him satisfy my hunger and quench my thirst."

There is something refreshingly healthy about wishing for childlike faith and simplicity again. Jesus said that without such a mentality we could not enter the kingdom of heaven (Matt. 18:3). A macro principle in the Next-Big-Thing lifestyle is to remember what we have been saved from. Isaiah said, "Look to the rock from which you were cut and to the quarry from which you were hewn…" (Isa. 51:1). This is one of the reasons those in the early church shared the Lord's Supper once a week. It helped them to slow down and to remember the Cross and what had been done for them and not to substitute hyper-works for humble worship. The church of Ephesus was a hard-working, persevering church that put to the test and identified false prophets and endured many hardships. They succeeded in hating "the practices of the Nicolaitans…" (Rev. 2:6) but had failed in loving Jesus. They were good haters but bad lovers. They needed to remember their first love.

Repent

"Repent and do the things you did at first. If you do not repent, I will come to you and remove your lamp stand from its place" (Revelation 2:5).

Bob Dylan once sang, "I'm gonna change my way of thinkin' – live by a whole new set of rules." To repent simply means to change the way you think. It's an open acknowledgment that you are going the wrong way, and a commitment to do a 180-degree turn and head in the right direction, the way God has pointed out. The Ephesian church got a clear word from the Lord about what was wrong. They now had to repent and start pursuing their first love once again.

Repentance always boils down to a choice. Will we respond to the truth revealed to us by the Holy Spirit or will we go our own way? In the case of the Ephesians they were good at condemning sin but not so good at loving sinners. That had to change. I think the late Darryl

Walker faced a similar choice in his ministry as a street evangelist in San Francisco.

A few years ago I was privileged to have a long conversation about Jesus with one of the leaders of the gay community in San Francisco. Our talk shifted to the topic of Darryl Walker who had been killed in a motorcycle accident just a few weeks before. When I said that I had heard that many leaders of the gay community were at Darryl's funeral, the leader said to me with a great tenderness in his voice, "We in the gay community did not agree with Darryl. We did not like his stance on our lifestyle. But the reason many of us attended his funeral was that there was one thing we knew about Darryl Walker, and that was that he loved us." Darryl never stopped sweating the small stuff and in an arena where the church's reputation is not primarily characterized by love, Darryl Walker stood out as a beautiful exception. He didn't change his mind about truth. He did changed it with love.

Repeat

"... do the things you did at first" (Revelation 2:5).

After Jesus rebuked the Ephesian church for having forsaken the basics, He challenged them to repeat the works they did at the first. When we begin our walk with

Jesus our initial acts of obedience to God often lay a firm foundation on which God builds future faith. King David warned that even godly foundations can be destroyed (Ps.11:3). So to prevent that, God gave us an illustration in what the prophet Amos called the divine plumbline (Amos 7:7-9). This combination of the Word and Spirit allows us to make sure our spiritual "house" is aligned with its foundations. Returning to our Next-Big-Thing hero from chapter one, it was Ananias who told Paul what his "first works" would be (Acts 9:16). Paul would refer back to that foundation-laying time regularly (Acts 22:12-15, 26:16-20).

Our first works are usually outward manifestations of our inward DNA – a spiritual genetic code that God has hard-wired into our souls. Much like the tribal identity of ancient Israel, God has placed us as individuals into spiritual tribes with leaders known for the distinctive of their foundational DNA. I often drink from the well of Chuck Smith, who founded the Calvary Chapel movement that gave me a heart for the Scriptures. Loren Cunningham, George Verwer, and other missions

> *Our first works are usually outward manifestations of our inward DNA – a spiritual genetic code that God has hard-wired into our souls.*

leaders impacted me with their heart for the world. Not only their teaching (information) but their impartation (formation) is reflected in my life today. It's these foundations that I return to when I stray away from the Next-Big-Thing lifestyle.

Sadly, we must beware because even great movements can stray from their foundational DNA. How many Methodists would benefit beyond their wildest dreams if they would simply model and repeat the works of their denomination's spiritual father, John Wesley. His methodical (hence the term Methodists) disciplines and teachings on prayer, fasting, evangelism, holiness, and small group discipleship transformed England. His writings on the social issues of the day such as slavery, working man's rights, sea piracy, etc. showed a deep moral concern for his nation. This was based on an uncompromising commitment to the Bible as God's Word.

Today, the denomination still has a strong concern for social issues, but they have drifted from the biblical foundations that anchored them. In a survey published in his book *Religion in Radical Transition,* sociologist Jeffrey Hadden reports that only thirteen percent of today's Methodist ministers believe that the Bible is "the inspired Word and inerrant Word of God." A similar challenge could be given to the heirs of Lutheran, Presbyterian,

Anglican, Salvation Army, and other denominations. Are they doing the works of Luther, Calvin, Cranmer and the Booths? No matter what movement reflects your spiritual heritage, the question is, are you displaying the spiritual DNA that God put in to your movement when it was born? First works are linked with first love. Doing them is a key to making our journey back to first-love living.

Return

"Return to me, for I have redeemed you" (Isa. 44:22).

God's longing to have His people return to Him is a theme that resonates through all the prophetic books of the Bible and into the New Testament. God knows we are prone to wander, to turn our hearts to other things. But as a loving Father, He doesn't give up on us. He keeps whispering to His sons and daughters, "Return to me." Consider this expression of His heart from the prophet Jeremiah:

"Go, proclaim this message toward the north: 'Return, faithless Israel,' declares the LORD, 'I will frown on you no longer, for I am faithful,' declares the LORD, 'I will not be angry forever'"(Jer. 3:11-13).

The Church at Ephesus had turned away from their first love (Jesus). In reminding them of this in Revelation 2, the Lord was giving them an opportunity to return to Him and be restored to full and fruitful relationship.

Going the Extra Inch

Writing this book has made me increasingly aware of just how big our little acts of kindness count up for God's kingdom. One example is the story of a missionary friend who has faithfully served in Southeast Asia for twenty years. Once, while in a severe trial, he was ready to quit and desperately needed counsel. At a missions conference he set up an appointment with a high-ranking missionary leader. Before they met, he said to himself, "If this leader ignores me or once looks at his watch – I'm done!" To his surprise, the leader showed him genuine fatherly love. The leader extended the session an extra hour, maintained eye contact, punctuated the session with a few jokes, and treated him as if they were old friends. And not once did he look at his watch!

These small gestures, though not calculated or planned by this leader, were but a natural outgrowth of his Next-Big-Thing lifestyle. They helped bring healing to a hurting person, restored his trust in authority figures and extended the man's missionary career. His leader did a small thing with great love. Mother Teresa once said,

"We cannot do great things, only small things with great love." Little things matter.

Author John Maxwell speaks of "adding value" to people we meet even if only for a few moments. Using a banking metaphor, he says we either make a deposit or a withdrawal with every encounter. He encourages us to always have on hand a large quantity of deposit slips!

Mother Teresa once said, "We cannot do great things, only small things with great love."

Once, after a meeting at which I had spoken, several people came forward for prayer. While talking with one lady after the meeting, she said she attended Applegate Christian Fellowship, a large church in Medford, Oregon. I'll never forget her comment about Jon Courson, Applegate's pastor. "After church Jon always greets the hundreds of worshippers coming out the door. With such a large church it would be understandable for the pastor to rush through his greetings and obligatory handshakes. But whenever I approached him at the end of service he always made me feel that I was the most important person on the planet. He would fold his big arms around his Bible, look at and listen to me intently and not allow himself to be distracted by others waiting to speak with him. I felt like I was his best friend." When I heard this testimony

I thought, "Big church, little kindnesses – maybe there is a connection!"

Stories like these cause me to ponder my deposit/withdrawal ratio in my relationships and interaction with people. I have observed that my friend, youth evangelist Winkie Pratney is always the last person to leave a youth meeting and will give his time and energy to young people until the janitor turns out the lights. He never lets anyone else pick up the tab at the restaurant! He is a shining example of someone, who though in his sixties, maintains a childlike, joyful, grace-filled, love for Jesus. Not only has Winkie been a mentor to me in fueling my fire for evangelism and revival, but by his example causes me to say (though not out loud), "When I grow up I want to be like Winkie – the world's oldest living teenager!"

One of the relational challenges we face today in showing value to people is in our use of cell phones. These phones are a valuable ministry tool, but I have been on both the giving and receiving end of missed opportunities to make deposits in people's lives due to cell phone interruptions. After visibly wounding several people with my insensitivity, I've come up with a few rules of cell phone etiquette:

When entering a conversation with someone, I ask for a ten second "time out" to turn off my cell phone. This says to them that I value them and my time with them and that I don't want anything to interrupt us. If you forget the first rule and your phone rings, reach down and turn it off without looking at the screen to see who the call is from. This shields them from the awkward position of making them feeling rejected if, after you identify the caller, you choose to talk to the caller over them. Again you are adding value to your friend. If you are expecting an important call and can't in good conscience turn off the phone, ask forgiveness before you get far into the conversation. Say something like, "I'm expecting an important call, so please forgive me if my cell phone interrupts us."

We must realize that in our fast-paced, techno/info-driven world that people are still people. I remember a conversation I had a few years ago with Dan Kimball, who now pastors the innovative Vintage Faith Church. He spends most of his time trying to figure out how to connect the vintage Gospel with ever-changing generations of technologically shaped and marginalized young people. He described his journey from the light shows and smoke

> *Dan told me that his journey had taken him into more of a "low tech/high touch" approach to ministry, rather than trusting in the bells and whistles of modern technology.*

bombs of the nineties to pioneering his "Graceland" ministry among counter-cultural punks, Goths, leftists and gays in Santa Cruz, California. Dan told me that his journey had taken him into more of a "low tech/high touch" approach to ministry, rather than trusting in the bells and whistles of modern technology.

What Dan was saying is that, even though emerging generations seem hopelessly transfixed by the flickering pixels of their various lighted screens, they are still hungering for an impartation of truth and love to a new generation within a culture that is becoming increasingly impersonal.

During my yearly "Fast and Focus" days (see chapter 6), I ask God for strategies to help me go a few extra inches during the year. This intentional *kaizen* is one way to proactively love my neighbor. The list below may resemble New Year's resolutions, but they are in fact God-given ways to sweat the small stuff and thereby add value to people. Here is my personal list:

1. Call a different old friend once a week, especially tracking down those I've lost contact with.

2. Write personal cards (not emails!) to people who have blessed you. Even more so now, people appreciate going to the mail box and finding a personal note amidst the bills, newsletters, and junk mail.

3. Send gifts to people. I am constantly looking for good deals on items that build up believers in their faith. I love to bless unsuspecting friends and acquaintances by mailing them a good book, worship CD, Prayer Diary, or painting.

4. Get verbal. Just come out and tell people how much I love and appreciate them. Some of the most meaningful affirmations I've ever received have come from Joy Dawson, who is truly a "mother in Israel" to thousands of people worldwide. Despite suffering chronic back pain, Joy constantly seeks God, studies His Word, and encourages His people. On more than one occasion, she has looked at me with those burning prophetic eyes and said, "Do you know the deeeeeeeeep admiration, love and respect I have for you?" I could go for months on the strength of one compliment from Joy. She is so much like Jesus.

5. Give E-encouragement. I confess I'm still learning this one. When Facebook was first taking off I resisted joining. Frankly, I figured if I added up all the useless trivia my "friends" would send me, I would be wasting a lot of time. My wife Linda has changed my mind on this one. She is a

relentless encourager to hundreds on Facebook! She prays for and often sends uplifting words to the six friends whose pictures are randomly displayed every day on the left side of the page. She also passes along spiritually uplifting video clips, blogs, podcasts, poems, quotes, and jokes to hundreds of friends. With her, a little encouragement goes a long way.

Above all, be grateful for blessings large and small. In a world that is becoming increasingly cold and impersonal, we can make a big impression through what author Alexander McCall Smith calls, *The Lost Art of Gratitude* and practice what TV personality Deborah Norville calls, *Thank You Power.* Three seconds of gratefulness could make the day for a waitress, store clerk, flight attendant, or anyone else who has been kind to you.

Again, here is where my wife Linda has been such a great example. Recently we had an incredible hassle registering a car that we had purchased from a less-than-honest person. We spent a whole day straightening out the mess at the Department of Motor Vehicles, Satellite City Hall, District Court, and back again. Then we met two Hawaiian ladies who went the extra inch for us and made a tough day a little better. Afterward, Linda took time to track them down, and tell them how thankful we were. I once asked Loren Cunningham, YWAM's founder, what was the one quality he appreciated most about his wife Darlene. Without blinking an eye he said, "She's the most grateful person that I know."

The Bible plainly says, "…give thanks in all circumstances…" (1 Thess. 5:17). Both the Old and New Testaments repeatedly exhort us to be grateful and give plenty of good reasons for doing so. King David even sang that we enter His gates with thanksgiving and His courts with praise (Ps. 100:4). You show me a bummed out, joyless Christian, and I'll show you a thankless Christian. Gratefulness to God and to others breeds contentment and joy.

> *Both Old and New Testaments repeatedly exhort us to be grateful and give plenty of good reasons for doing so.*

The same God who gives us the heavenly sky shows each evening, also dreamed up the beautiful, intricate, artistic designs on the smallest of insects. Both by command and example He expects us to sweat the small stuff.

Experience the joy in making someone else's day (or perhaps their life!) by going the extra inch. And you know what? You just might make God's day too!

9

NO LITTLE PEOPLE, NO LITTLE PLACES

"The Scripture emphasizes that little can become much if the little is truly consecrated to God. There are no little people and big people in the true spiritual sense, but only consecrated and unconsecrated people." – Francis Schaeffer

On December 28th, 2004, I was sitting in the parking lot of a Christian bookstore in Sacramento, California, browsing through my newly-purchased books, compliments of a Christmas present from my mother-in-law. My cell phone rang and the other end of the line was Tim Svoboda, at that time director of YWAM's missionary work in southern India.

"Danny, have you heard about the tsunami?"

"Of course I have. There's been nothing else on the TV for the last two days. How can I help?"

"We need money," Tim replied, "lots of it... We're gathering dead bodies, praying for people and looking for shelters for the homeless all along the Chennai coast. We need 60,000 dollars right now and we'll need at least a quarter of a million dollars in the next two months to buy new carts for peanut salesmen, new boats for the fishermen, and to rebuild homes for the poor. We've got workers on the ground ready to go but we need money." I said goodbye with a wimpy, "I'll do my best."

Staring out the car window, I could visualize Indian women and children weeping over the loss of husbands and fathers. I saw thousands of people homeless and YWAMers scurrying to help with very few resources. Then unbelief flooded my soul. You see, I've never been a great fundraiser. I put my head on the steering wheel and said my favorite prayer, "Help, Lord." It was then I felt God's still small voice speak to my heart: "What's in your hand?" I looked down and said, "My cell phone." I remembered that God once asked Moses the same question when he was carrying a rod – a rod that was to become the rod of God (Exodus 4:2).

Moses tended sheep for forty years, and a key tool in the shepherd's trade was a rod. The rod that God had given Moses to steer sheep in the right direction was also a guidance tool to lead the children of Israel out of bondage and into God's Promise Land. In addition, it was used as an instrument of judgment upon the Egyptians.

My Blackberry became the cell phone of God! Sitting there in the parking lot, I called pastors and friends asking for money to help with the tsunami relief work. I also called KLHT radio in Honolulu where I broadcast a regular missions-focused program, to ask if I could make an appeal on the radio. To make a long story short, within three weeks over 350,000 dollars were raised and used to help minister to thousands of needy people in India!

A cell phone is a *little* thing. But as Dr. Schaeffer said, there are no little or big things with God, simply consecrated and unconsecrated things.

Writing to the Corinthians, Paul gave them what has become our most well-known metaphor for the people of God – the body of Christ. He then pursued the word picture in more detail by referring to smaller body parts such as feet, hands, eyes, ears and head.

A cell phone is a little thing. But as Dr. Schaeffer said, there are no little or big things with God, simply consecrated and unconsecrated things.

"On the contrary, those parts of the body that seem to be weaker are indispensable, and the parts that we think are less honorable we treat with special honor. And the parts that are unpresentable are treated with special modesty, while our presentable parts need no special treatment, but God has combined the members of the body and has given greater honor to the parts that lacked it, so that there should be no division in the body but that its parts should have equal concern for each other. If one part suffers, every part suffers with it; if one part is honored, every part rejoices with it. Now you are the body of Christ, and each one of you is a part of it" (1 Cor. 12:22-27). The application is clear: a speck of sand in the eye or an ingrown toe nail, though small maladies, can greatly hinder the function of the whole body. Hence the need to recognize even the little members of the body as "indispensable."

> *...a speck of sand in the eye or an ingrown toe nail, though small maladies, can greatly hinder the function of the whole body.*

You need not be a mathematician to project what could happen in world evangelization, discipling the nations, serving the poor and the needy, and fighting injustice, if every part of the body was to function in its proper place, whether it be big or little. Unfortunately, American churches reportedly have the same 80/20 service ratio as secular organizations, meaning twenty percent of the people do eighty percent of the work and vice-versa. Furthermore, the average Christian tithes around three percent of his finances away and the average church gives about that percentage to missionary work (perhaps there is a connection here?).

In Revelation 3:8, Jesus told the church of Philadelphia to use their "little strength" and go through the doors he would open for them. In other words, be faithful in the little, and I will make you ruler over much (Lk. 16:10). If each of us would simply serve in the little place that God has called us, when multiplied by the service of the half-billion born-again Christians, there would be no limit to what we could accomplish. To examine the "Big Picture," I want us to put away our telescopes temporarily and get out our microscopes to look at the little things we could be doing to further the cause of Christ.

Therese of Lisieux, a nineteenth century Carmelite nun described her devotion to God as "The Little Way." She taught a path to true holiness revolving around "trifles" – small acts of kindness especially to those who annoy us, welcoming unjust criticisms, and helping those who are ungrateful, and seeking out menial jobs. Her deceptively simple "Little

> *We may think that these trivial pursuits are hardly worth giving attention to, but that is precisely their value. They give opportunities for little victories over the Goliath in all of us – the giant of selfishness.*

Way" can be practiced by anyone in any calling in life. We may think that these trivial pursuits are hardly worth giving attention to, but that is precisely their value. They give opportunities for little victories over the Goliath in all of us – the giant of selfishness.

In Paul's letter to the Ephesians, he describes the church as "God's workmanship" – a masterpiece by a Master artist who is painting our lives after His image (Eph. 2:10). Paul saw clearly that the original design God had for us would reflect true beauty as His grace and gifts are used for good works. What is your rod? What time, talents, and treasures has He given you that you in turn can consecrate to Him?

The Fine Wine of Kindness

Not long ago, on a flight from Honolulu to Chicago, I was providentially seated next to Ali, a distinguished Middle Eastern man who looked to be in his early seventies. As Ali took his place in the aisle seat, he noticed my Bible on the tray table in front of me. He then reached in his carry-on bag and pulled out a Qur'an. We both smiled, knowing we were in for an interesting flight! For hours we discussed theology, politics, terrorism, and both learned from one another as we tried to convert each other.

Ali and I soon established some common ground: He had a religious book (the Qur'an); I had a religious book (the Bible); He had a name for God (Allah); I had a name for God (Yahweh). He had a prophet (Mohammed); I had a prophet (Jesus). I knew that Jesus was more than a prophet. However, I always try to remember the counsel of my Egyptian friend Samy Tanagho, when presenting the Gospel to Muslims, not give "too much – too soon".

As Ali and I sipped on orange juice, we began to discuss the character of God. I told him that the Bible agreed with Islam's daily proclamation that, "God is great" (Ps. 48:1). I then said, "You know, Ali, we also believe, as you do, that God is all powerful. However, we don't believe that it is primarily God's power that saves us." I then turned to Romans 2:4, which says, "God's kindness leads you toward repentance." I then talked about the Cross. Ali told me that he had seen *The Passion of the Christ* movie and was familiar with the Gospel message. So I turned up the heat.

"God could have squeezed us into submission by virtue of His great power. But instead, He took the opposite road of humility and submission. Christ's death on the Cross demonstrated God's kindness in forgiving the sins of people who did not deserve it. Now with Jesus' arms wide open, He calls all who will from every nation to come to Him. He knows that if anything would draw men and women of their own free will to repent, it would surely be the loving-kindness demonstrated on the Cross."

I could see that the penny had dropped, so to speak, and Ali took a double take as the magnetism of God's kindness began to grab a hold of his heart.

I wish I could report to you that Ali gave his life to Christ on the plane that day. He didn't. He had been teaching Islamic studies for years at a university back East. He had emigrated from Lebanon as a young man and staunchly held on to his Islamic beliefs. I wasn't going to crack that in an eight-hour flight. The Lord used it, however, to draw him closer to Christ and also to teach me a lesson about the kindness of God.

It is here that we find one of the major keys to a Next-Big-Thing lifestyle. If you were to ask most Christians to give a one-word definition of God, most would say "love." This would be based not only on a general perception of God but a direct statement made by the Apostle John, "God is love" (1 Jn. 4:16). However, when seeking to define love, the definitions tend to dissolve into sloppy sentimentalism. Sometimes our inadequate descriptions of the majesty of God's love are no better than those of the Beatles when they said, "All you need is love" (and shortly thereafter broke up)!

I once did a study on the concept of God's love for sinners and found that almost every time this topic is mentioned in Scripture it is connected with what Christ did on the Cross. The love of God in the Bible is not an abstract proposition, but a foundation for action that demonstrates the true nature of

...our inadequate descriptions of the majesty of God's love are no better than those of the Beatles when they said, "All you need is love" (and shortly thereafter broke up)!

love. A better description comes from the Hebrew word *Hesed*, which is most accurately translated loving-kindness. Over thirty times in the Old Testament "*Hesed*" is listed as a key attribute of God. God's loving-kindness is said to be good, marvelous, great, excellent, merciful, everlasting, and better than life in various biblical descriptions. *Hesed* is not only an essential and distinctive quality of God, but it should characterize God's people as well (Hosea 4:1, 12:6, Micah 6:8).

The New Testament writers chose the word "*Chrestos*" as a definition of this loving-kindness of God. They borrowed the word from classic Greek in which *Chrestos* was used to determine good, fine-aged wine. Jesus used it this way in his parable of the wineskins when he said, "The old wine is better (*Chrestos*)" (Luke 5:39).

When I was in my teens, I spent many Friday and Saturday nights hiding in the shadows near Z's Liquor Store on Pleasure Point in Santa Cruz, California. Since I was not of legal drinking age, I would ask older customers to score me some cheap wine for my weekend partying. My opening line was, "Hey, bro, can you score me some Red Ripple?" The phrase "rot-gut" aptly describes its effects on my stomach, and I look back with laughter and embarrassment at the nights I spent heaving over many toilet bowls due to my attempts to get drunk on the cheap. When I gave my life to Christ and drank freely of the *Chrestos* of God, I never wanted the world's cheap wine again. What a difference in "taste" there is between Christians who pour out His loving-kindness and the rot-gut feeling we get from people who are unloving, unkind, critical, judgmental, and otherwise nasty. The "aftertaste" we leave with others should make them satisfied and wanting to come back for more. This is a Next-Big-Thing attitude that needs to be nurtured in every believer.

First Corinthians 13 makes it crystal clear that if we don't have God's love we are nothing. Over the years, I have met hundreds of evangelists, teachers, and musicians, and it doesn't take long to spot those who reflect God's *Chrestos* and those who do not. The marks of godly leadership are humility, servanthood, and genuine concern for people. Stories of the opulence and arrogance of Christian superstars are legendary and unfortunately many of these stories are not exaggerated. A spirit of selfishness and pride quickly exposes them as the prima donnas they are.

One of the most popular teachers in our YWAM Discipleship Training Schools is Art Collins. Ask many people in the YWAM world about Art and they will laugh and say, "I know him – the donut guy!" Whenever Art teaches, he brings donuts to class and shares them freely with the students. He also hands out New Testaments and takes his students out for pizza. You may suggest that he's bribing the students with his goodies, but I call it a demonstration of the loving-kindness of God that reinforces his teaching on servanthood. Where does he get his money for these acts of generosity? He uses the honorariums that are

...studies have shown that nice people have a lower divorce rate, make more money, are healthier, and spend less time in lawsuits than people who are not "nice."

given him and saves some to use in the non-Western world where he does not receive speaker honorariums. Art is one of my heroes!

In their best-selling book, *The Power of Nice,* Thaler and Koval demonstrate that even in general society, studies have shown that nice people have a lower divorce rate, make more money, are healthier, and spend less time in lawsuits than people who are not "nice." To quote them, "it is often the small kindnesses – the smiles, gestures, compliments and favors that make our day and can even change our lives." The authors disagree with the famous quote by major league baseball manager Leo Durocher: "Nice guys finish last." The authors go on to say, "Nice not only finishes first; those who use its nurturing power wind up happier to boot!"

Pastor Ralph Moore has overseen the startup of over forty churches in Hawaii and hundreds more overseas through his Hope Chapel movement. Whenever a pastor from another denomination moves into Ralph's "territory" and approaches Ralph to inform him of their intention to start a church near one of his churches, Ralph's consistent response is, "How much money do you need? Can I give you some of my people? And can I introduce you to key contacts in the area?" The motto for Hope Chapel churches is: "We Promise to Love You, as You Are," because that is the nature of God, the spirit of Jesus and a demonstration of God's *Chrestos* – fine wine indeed.

Melissa Etheridge, a popular singer also well-known for her gay lifestyle, encouraged everyone on her website to get behind Pastor Rick Warren's initiatives to alleviate the suffering of AIDS victims in Africa. Why, you may ask, would a homosexual activist encourage her constituents to support an evangelical pastor who encouraged his people to vote against California's gay marriage initiative? It is simply because Rick showed her loving-kindness. When they were scheduled to speak together at the same event, they chatted before going on stage. Rick Warren told Melissa how much he appreciated her music. He talked about his wife's battle with breast cancer (Ms. Etheridge had been a cancer victim just a few years before). He also shared about his commitment to fight AIDS in Africa. They found a commonality in suffering and a friendship was born between them. Perhaps Melissa is a tad more open to the Gospel of Christ than she would have been before Warren's act of kindness to her.

What would happen in our world today if Christians were known for what we were for and the acts of kindness that we did, rather than for what we were against and the deeds of darkness that we condemn? Loving-kindness – another key component of the Next-Big-Thing lifestyle.

10

THE BIG PICTURE: WHAT ON EARTH IS THE KINGDOM OF HEAVEN?

So by now you get it. The Next-Big-Thing lifestyle is simply being faithful to the next thing God tells you to do. If we stray from God's freeway, He invites us to return to the exit ramp and get back on, by obeying Him in that last small or big thing He directed us to do. The Next Big Thing emphasizes character – cultivating humility, contentment, and faithfulness as the dominating virtues of our lives. The thesis in a nutshell: When we are faithful in the big and little things, we can count on Him to take care of our lot in life (our *kuleana* – see Chapter 5).

It is also important for us to see the "big picture" of God's purpose for the whole world. All our big and small efforts are building His kingdom on earth. His ultimate intention is to gather all things together as one in Christ (Eph. 1:10).

After telling His disciples the parable of the sower, Jesus gives a rather cryptic explanation of why He used parables in His teaching. "This is why I speak to them in parables, though seeing, they do not see; though hearing they do not hear or understand" (Matt. 13:13). He then quoted Isaiah to further illustrate the point I have been making: When we harden our hearts, He stops speaking. When we are faithful to obey what we hear, He entrusts us with more. As this parable and subsequent parables show, God wants the seeds we sow to grow and be an influence in our world. We must not forget, however, that this influence is in reference to what Jesus called the kingdom of heaven.

In the four Gospels (Matthew, Mark, Luke, and John), the terms kingdom of heaven and the kingdom of God are synonymous. We know this by simply comparing parallel passages in the four Gospels. The kingdom was Jesus' core message and the thrust of the whole Bible. We need to understand this kingdom so we can know how we seek it, pray for it to come, and enter it (Matt. 6:10, 33, 18:3). Hence we will conclude our focus on the Next Big Thing with the ultimate and last Big Thing on God's agenda – the kingdom of heaven and how it is to be manifested on earth.

Jesus said that His disciples were to be the salt of the earth as well as the light of the world. Christians throughout history have agreed that the "light" metaphor referred to the light of the Gospel going into the darkness of the world and men's hearts (2 Cor. 4:5-6). They are likewise in agreement that the "salt" word picture refers to the preserving effect His disciples were to have in the world, restraining evil.

Once again, these kingdom terms are not in conflict, but represent a holistic approach of loving our neighbor (salt) and bring the good news of salvation (light).

Salvation Army founder William Booth once cautioned his soldiers not to preach to someone with a toothache. He reasoned that their dental pain was so loud they wouldn't be able to hear the Gospel. His remedy: fix the tooth then get 'em saved!

Is it possible to go to one extreme and just try to "pitchfork souls into heaven" and not care about people in the here and the now? Yes. Is it possible, on the other hand, to go to the extreme of trying to build God's kingdom on earth, redeem social structures and make this world a happy place while in the end most people go to hell? Again, yes. Why must we go to extremes? Why not try to come up with a healthy understanding of God's kingdom using the whole Bible as our paradigm and go into all the world seeking, praying for, and entering God's kingdom?

Returning to Matthew 13, Jesus continued to give various metaphors describing the kingdom of heaven. He told the parable of the weeds to illustrate the reality of the wheat (good seed) growing side by side with the weeds (bad seed) and the inevitability of them being linked together at their roots. Hence, the need to wait for God to separate them. He then went on to illustrate what we have been talking about in this book so far, and that is, little things like mustard seeds and particles of yeast, though they be so small, can grow into a giant tree and a loaf of bread respectively (Matt 13:31-33).

The Value of Values

Jesus then went on to give two stories illustrating the value of the kingdom of heaven. In the first, a man discovers a hidden treasure and upon seeing its value, sells all that he has to purchase the land on which he found it. In the second, a pearl merchant is looking for fine pearls, and when he finds one of "great value," he sells everything to buy this "pearl of great price" (Matt. 13:44-46 KJV). These two "value parables" differ in some detail (in the treasure story the man just happens to find the treasure and in the pearl story the man is looking for valuable pearls). They however, still illustrate the same point: Once we understand the value of the kingdom of heaven, nothing else in our lives will do.

The intent of these parables is simple. It is to point out that we will give our lives to what we esteem to be of value. As a boy, Tiger Woods tacked a poster of Jack Nicholas on his bedroom wall because his life goal was to go after all of Jack Nicholas' records and become the greatest golfer in the world. Unfortunately, Tiger failed to value his marriage with the same passion, and he has had to pay the consequences.

Jesus and the New Testament writers went to great pains to explain that even though the Old Testament law was intended to change our values, it lacked the power to change our hearts. Hence, the outpouring of the Holy Spirit on the Day of Pentecost (Acts 2) was needed to give us the power to love the things of true value rather than counterfeits that distract us from the ultimate value – Christ and His kingdom.

> *Jesus and the New Testament writers went to great pains to explain that even though the Old Testament law was intended to change our values, it lacked the power to change our hearts.*

At the conclusion of Jesus' masterful painting of the kingdom of heaven through His various stories, He injects a bit of timeless wisdom: "Therefore every teacher of the law who has been instructed about the kingdom of heaven is like the owner of the house who brings out of his store-room new treasures as well as old" (Matt. 13:52). Here He uses a value word again – treasure – and tells us that this kingdom of heaven has both old and new treasures, and the wise student will draw on both.

Paul gave a similar instruction to the church of Ephesus when he prayed for them in the opening chapter of his letter to them: "I keep asking the God of our Lord Jesus Christ, the glorious Father, may give you the spirit of *wisdom and revelation* so that you may know him better. I pray also the eyes of your heart maybe enlightened that you may know the hope to which He has called you, the riches of his glorious inheritance in the saints and his incomparably great power for us who believe…" (Eph. 1:17-18).

Although Paul didn't use kingdom terminology in his letter to the Ephesians, he is in essence giving the same instructions that Jesus did. In the Next-Big-Thing lifestyle, we reach into the treasure of the "old" wisdom discovered by those who have gone before us. This valuing of teaching by great men and women of faith anchors our new revelation with the church's foundations while embracing God's unfolding kingdom agenda.

As Moses passed the baton of leadership to Joshua and a new generation of Israelites, he urged them not to forget their heritage: "Remember the days of old; consider the generations long past. Ask your father and he will tell you, your elders and they will explain it to you" (Deut. 32:7). Likewise, as we round the homestretch of world history before Christ returns, let's glean as much wisdom as possible from our elders while we seek God for revival in our generation.

Likewise, as we round the homestretch of world history before Christ returns, let's glean as much wisdom as possible from our elders while we seek God for revival in our generation.

With this as our background, I would like to take you on a short tour of church history and examine some spiritual giants who have gone before us. What we learn from their example, we can apply in our time.

Paul's "Urgent" and Primary Instruction

In Paul's first letter to Timothy, he exhorted his young protégé to lead the church of Ephesus into God's eternal purpose. He urged them: "…of primary importance…" to pray for secular rulers – those in the governmental sphere. Why? So that we could live "…peaceful and quiet lives…" Why? "…because this is good, and pleases God our

Savior." Why? "...because God wants all men to be saved and come to the knowledge of the truth." Why? "For there is one God and one mediator between God and men, the man Christ Jesus." Paul then goes on to describe the extent of Jesus "ransom" for all men (1 Tim. 2:1-6).

I humbly submit a simple interpretation and application of this passage: We are to pray for all men and "all those that are in authority" because they control the social structures that allow us to lead peaceful lives. These are the structures of the church, the home, government, education, art, sports, entertainment and the media. To borrow a metaphor, these are the gates of the city. The primary prayer is not for salvation, but for an atmosphere of tranquility and godliness in which leaders give us basic civil liberties. The Founding Fathers of the United States understood this from the biblical worldview emerging in Western Europe because

> *We cannot separate Christianity's influence on social structures any more than we can "pitchfork souls into heaven" and therefore Christians need to be both the salt of the earth as well as the light of the world.*

of Christianity's influence. The progression in this text indicates that a peaceful atmosphere paves the way for dissemination of the Gospel for "all people to be saved and to come to a knowledge of the truth" (v. 4).

We cannot separate Christianity's influence on social structures any more than we can "pitchfork souls into heaven" and therefore Christians need to be both the salt of the earth as well as the light of the world. In fact, the more effective we are as salt, the brighter our light will be. Throughout church history gospel-preaching, Bible-believing missionaries, and church planters have been the most effective at initiating social and cultural change in the nations. Below is a random sampling:

Tertullian in the third century wrote, "Christians sup-. port and bury people...support boys and girls who are destitute of parents...old people and those who have suffered shipwreck or are shut up in prison."

In the Middle Ages, the monastic movements promoted scholarly learning as well as agricultural advances. Historian Thomas Cahill credits Irish monks with "saving civilization" by copying great works of literature as well as the Scriptures.

Other historians believe John Wesley, the great British evangelist and church planter, saved England from a bloody revolution like the one endured by France. His preaching gave people hope amid times of great social unrest. He said, "Christianity is essentially a social religion.

To turn it into a solitary religion is to destroy it." A perusal of Wesley's sermons reveals his passion for what he called "national issues" of the day: wealth and poverty, war, education, medical ethics, sea piracy, free trade, slavery, and the liquor industry. He was also one of the greatest soul winners in history.

John Eliot, a missionary to the Algonquin Native Americans, preached the Gospel with zeal and translated the Bible into their language. In addition, he fought for justice and clemency for Indian prisoners, freedom for Indian slaves, and prevented Algonquins from being defrauded of their land. He also established schools for Indian children.

William Carey, "The Father of Modern Missions" and a pioneer missionary to India, introduced the steam engine, taught the locals how to produce their own paper for publishing, built the largest printing press in the nation, and established the first savings bank. He preached against bribery and labored for the humane treatment of lepers. He lobbied to change the law concerning suttee or widow burning (no doubt many widows were grateful for that one!). Carey taught economics, botany, agriculture, and mathematics. Furthermore, he won souls, planted churches, and translated the Bible into several Indian languages. WHEW!

Catherine Booth, William's wife and Salvation Army co-founder had a favorite reply when her contemporaries would try to draw her into controversy over their theology and practice: "My friends, all I know is that souls are dying, dying," she would exclaim with a passion for the perishing multitudes. The Salvation Army (which could never be criticized as being too heavenly-minded) began as a model of evangelism and social action working together. General Booth told his officers to, "Go for souls and go for the worst!" The Booths and their followers also fed the hungry, clothed the naked, sheltered the homeless, and worked against corruption in government. William's landmark book, *In Darkest England and the Way Out* outlined a plan to disciple the nation in dealing with its social problems. The Booths' driving passion, however, was the winning of the lost to Christ.

General Booth told his officers to, "Go for souls and go for the worst!"

In the Sandwich Islands (Hawaii), New England missionaries followed Carey's lead and served the people's practical as well as spiritual needs. They treated people suffering from diseases brought in by Western whaling ships. They started schools to provide educational opportunities for the Hawaiian people. They also translated the

Bible and other books into the Hawaiian language. The result – the largest church in the world in 1839 was in Hilo, Hawaii and a larger percentage of Hawaiians became Christians than any other nation per capita in church history.

I could go on giving illustrations to back up my thesis that our posture toward the kingdom of heaven is not an either/or proposition (*either* heaven or earth). It is *both* heaven and earth. The people who have discipled the nations best were those who put the preaching of the Gospel first. They labored to establish their converts as obedient disciples of Jesus and taught both the social and individual commands of the Gospel. Missionary Statesman E. Stanley Jones said, "An individual Gospel without a social Gospel is like a soul without a body. A social Gospel without an individual Gospel is like a body without a soul. The one is a ghost and the other is a corpse. Put the two together and you have a living person."

> *The people who have discipled the nations best were those who put the preaching of the Gospel first.*

So as we plant our little mustard seed, God wants us to have a Big Picture vision of the tree that will grow from it and the birds that will rest in its branches. For the day is coming when the kingdom of heaven will fill the whole earth. The prophet Daniel, gave us the following description of God's future kingdom: "In the time of those kings the God of heaven will set up a kingdom that will never be destroyed nor will it be left to another people. It will crush all those kingdoms and bring them to an end but it will itself endure forever" (Dan. 2:44). This is the promise that we have. This is the Big Picture. God's kingdom is the ultimate Next Big Thing.

Solomon closed the book of Ecclesiasties with these words, "Fear God and keep his commandments, for this is the whole duty of man. For God will bring every deed into judgment, including every hidden thing, whether it is good or evil" (Ecc. 12:12-14). Solomon talked about a lot of issues in his great book, but the bottom line is we should simply keep God's commandments and do the next thing He tells us to do.

In this book, the most powerful image is the butterfly. Only God knows how big or lasting the effects are of one flap of a butterfly's wings – whether simply affecting the trajectory of the butterfly next door or actually causing that tornado in Texas. God is in charge of the effects of our actions; we are simply in charge of doing the Next Big Thing.

In the early seventies I was a confused teenager sitting on a fence outside of Mueller's Bar on Washington

Boulevard in Baltimore. Out of nowhere, my father appeared from around the corner. Our eyes met. In our own way, each of us were trying to deal with the recent loss of my mom to cancer. Spontaneously he asked me, "What are you doing, Son?" To which I replied, "Waitin' for somthin' to happen!" Then with a lot of fatherly love and little prophetic punch he said, "Why don't you go out and make something happen?!"

Those words have resonated with me ever since then, especially at times when I am just "sittin' on a fence" of one kind or another, just waiting for something to happen. In many ways over the years my dad has been an inspiration to me to have a healthy disdain for "fence-sitting" and an obsession to do the Next Big Thing that God by His grace tells me to do.

So, dear reader, as we part ways, let me encourage you to have a strong distaste for the fence-sitting (or pew-sitting) inaction that is the lot of those who don't pursue the Next Big Thing. To use Jesus' term, don't settle for a "lukewarm" Christian life. Allow the power of the Holy Spirit to light a fire under you that neither the world, the flesh, nor the devil will be able to extinguish. The good news is that you don't have to wait to complete your education, get married, have a mentor, get a job (or quit one), sell your stocks, or change your diet. All you have to do is to slow down, listen to that still small Voice inside and do the next thing God tells you to do. The next thing is The Next Big Thing.

ABOUT THE AUTHOR

Danny Lehmann lives in Hawaii with his wife Linda. He is the leader of Youth With A Mission-Hawaii, serves on the Global Leadership Forum of YWAM International, and is the overseer of YWAM's Bible and missions schools worldwide as the Dean of the College of Christian Ministries.

While a surfer in California Danny was confronted with the Gospel on the beach and shortly thereafter converted to Christ. After a few months of rehabilitation and growing in the faith at Shekinah House (an outreach of Calvary Chapel Costa Mesa) he began to share his faith on the beaches and streets. He assisted in planting Mission Christian Fellowship and founded The Land, a Christian community emphasizing evangelism and discipleship.

In 1980 Danny joined Youth With A Mission and continued to lead outreach teams to the South Pacific and Asia. He was appointed Director of YWAM Honolulu in January 1983 and Director of YWAM Hawaii in 1988.

Danny has written three books on evangelism: *For the Gospel's Sake, Bringin' 'Em Back Alive,* and *Beautiful Feet.* In addition, he has written *Before You Hit the Wall,* a book about spiritual discipline; *Stoked! Firing Up Your Passion for God*, and various Gospel tracts.

He travels extensively teaching on evangelism, the disciplined life, and missions in various training schools and churches. He has been a teacher at Calvary Chapel Honolulu since 1983.

For materials to stoke your spiritual fire,
visit: www.stokerstuff.com
Or mail your order to:
Stoker Stuff
P.O. Box 61700
Honolulu, HI 96822

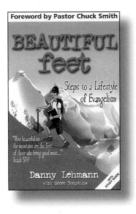

Evangelism, Witnessing, Missions. If these words strike fear in your heart, then this book is for you. Through practical illustrations, personal examples, and clear Bible teaching, Danny examines the Messengers, the Message, the Motives, and the Methods of evangelism. *Beautiful Feet* will help you to develop a lifestyle of evangelism.

Price $7.00 (includes shipping and handling)

Before You Hit the Wall: Shaping Up Spiritually to Win, is Danny Lehmann's current bestselling book. "The Wall" is that formidable obstacle that confronts marathon runners about half way through a race when they "run out of gas" and decide whether to drop out or press on to the finish.

In the spiritual race we face "The Wall" as well, through trials, testings and temptations. Will we give up and quit the race or will we press on to God's destiny for our lives? The answer lies in whether or not we, like marathon runners, have trained our souls through spiritual discipline. This book will help you discover practical ways so that the disciplined life is not only attainable, but enjoyable.

Price $7.00 (includes shipping and handling)

Are you stoked for Jesus? If you want the fire of God to burn in your soul, this book is for you! It's all about passion for God. In a time when religious compromise and half-hearted Christianity are more often the rule than the exception, Danny Lehmann teaches you how to rekindle a fiery passion for God and keep the fires stoked for years to come.

Stoked uses powerful illustrations from Scripture, personal insights, and stories from some of the most "stoked" Christians in history to draw readers closer to the heart of God. But beware. If you take its principles to heart, there's no way to avoid being set aflame by the all-consuming love of God.

Price $7.00 (includes shipping and handling)

The Facts of Life is an evangelistic tract that goes through four facts and how to receive Christ in a simple format:

1. God loves you and desires that you fulfill the destiny for which you were created.
2. We are separated from God because of our sins.
3. The penalty for our sins is death
4. Jesus Christ died, and rose again to save us from the power and penalty of sin.

What must I do? 1. Trust, 2. Turn, 3. Follow

The booklet contains good illustrations and simple explanations to give a clear gospel presentation.

Price $6.00 per pack of 25 (includes shipping and handling)